Copyright © 2016 by Dr. Martin Jones

All rights reserved. This book or any portion thereof may not be reproduced or used in any manner whatsoever without the express written permission of the publisher except for the use of brief quotations in a book review.

ISBN-13: 978-1539103035

ISBN-10: 153910303X

http://pythonforbiologists.com

Set in PT Serif and `Source Code Pro`

About the author

Martin started his programming career by learning Perl during the course of his PhD in evolutionary biology, and started teaching other people to program soon after. Since then he has taught introductory programming to hundreds of biologists, from undergraduates to PIs, and has maintained a philosophy that programming courses must be friendly, approachable, and practical.

In his academic career, Martin mixed research and teaching at the University of Edinburgh, culminating in a two year stint as Lecturer in Bioinformatics. He now runs programming courses for biological researchers as a full time freelancer.

You can get in touch with Martin at

martin@pythonforbiologists.com

Martin's other works include *Python for Biologists*, *Advanced Python for Biologists* and *Python for complete beginners*.

Table of Contents

1: Introduction — 1

About this book » 1
Typography and formatting » 5
Getting in touch » 8

2: Environments for developing in Python — 10

Introduction » 10
What you actually write code in » 10
Integrated development environments » 14
Managing Python and packages » 19
Working in a debugger » 25
Alternatives to pdb » 57
Recap » 59

3: Organizing and sharing code — 61

Introduction » 61
Working with modules » 63
Distributing code » 80
Recap » 86

4: Testing your code — 88

Introduction » 88
Testing with assert » 89
Automated testing with nose » 105
Types of assertions » 119
Designing for testing » 127
Special types of testing » 131
Recap » 137

5: Performance — 139

Introduction » 139
Benchmarking » 140
Benchmarking memory » 147

Profiling » 160
Guidelines for performance optimization » 179
Specific tips for improving performance » 181
Further topics in performance » 194
Recap » 197

6: Building user interfaces   198

Why do we need a user interface? » 198
A simple program » 200
A simple interactive interface » 203
A simple command line interface » 207
Command line interfaces with argparse » 216
Alternatives to argparse » 241
Configuration files » 243
Web interfaces » 250
Graphical user interfaces » 257
Logging » 269
Logging messages » 273
Logging to a file » 276
Recap » 283

1: Introduction

About this book

Biologists who have just finished learning the basics of Python often ask me the question: "What should I learn next?" One valid answer is to dive into the features of the Python language that might be considered more advanced – things like comprehensions, custom classes, and exception handling[1].

Another, slightly less obvious answer is to learn about the tools and techniques that exist in Python to make the process of developing software easier. These tend not to be core language features, but rather a collection of libraries, programs and approaches that solve problems that commonly occur when building scientific software. Questions like:

- How can I write code in less time?
- How do I share my code with other people?
- How do I make my code run faster?
- How do I make sure there aren't any errors in my code?
- How do I make my programs easier to use?

cannot be answered simply by pointing out different features of the Python language. Rather, they have to be answered by referring to the ecosystem of libraries and tools that have accumulated around Python.

These five questions form the basis of the five main chapters in this book. To learn how to write code more efficiently we will look at Python's choice

---

[1] My second book, *Advanced Python for Biologists*, represents my attempt to guide the biological programmer through those parts of the language.

of development environments. To learn how to share code, we'll investigate Python's packaging and distribution system. To make code faster and more reliable, we'll learn about profiling and automated testing. And to make our code usable by other people, we'll need to build user interfaces.

These five disparate topics all have three things in common. Firstly, they are not specific to Python: users of all programming languages struggle with similar problems, and often the Python solution draws inspiration from other programming communities.

Secondly, they are all large and complex – each chapter could easily form the basis for an entire book. However, they are also topics where a little bit of knowledge is extremely useful. It's a common rule of thumb in programming (and elsewhere) that 20% of the features of a given tool will allow you to do 80% of what you need[1]. It's my hope that this book will teach you the 20% of each topic – performance, distribution, testing, etc. – that you will use most often, and hence be more useful than a stack of five more specialized books.

Finally, all of the topics in this book involve not just new package and function names, but new ideas. To discuss performance we need to learn about *epochs* and *big O notation*; to understand testing we need to learn about *regressions* and *fixtures*; and to talk about sharing code we need to learn about *dependencies* and *namespaces*. You'll find that we spend a fair amount of time in each chapter looking at the basic ideas behind each topic, which will make life much easier when you eventually need to search for a feature or tool that isn't explicitly covered here.

---

[1] This idea is called the *Pareto Principle* and is found to apply to many fields.

Chapter 1:Introduction

How to use this book

Programming books generally fall into two categories; reference-type books, which are designed for looking up specific bits of information, and tutorial-type books, which are designed to be read cover-to-cover. This book is a bit of both: each chapter is intended to be read from start to finish, but the chapters themselves are relatively independent.

Within each chapter, we generally start off with a simple example and go into progressively more complex territory, so later sections of a given chapter won't make sense if you haven't read the earlier sections. This is particularly true of the chapters on building user interfaces and automated testing, both of which involve building up complex examples step by step. Where material from one chapter is relevant to another, I've tried to include references in footnotes.

Because the chapters are about very different topics, they differ quite a lot in both structure and content. Some chapters – like the one on building user interfaces– have a lot of code examples, while some – like the one on environments – have very few. Chapters which discuss a lot of command line tools naturally have a lot of examples of command line output; the chapter on performance is one such example.

Many of the techniques we'll discuss – notably things like automated testing, CPU profiling, and logging – are most useful when applied to larger programs. This presents a dilemma when it comes to writing examples for them: examples need to be small (in order to be easily understood, and to fit on the page) but small programs are the very ones for which the techniques are least useful! To counter this problem, I will ask you to use your imagination: when we are looking at small example programs, remember that they are standing in for the much large programs that we will write in the real world.

Because we will spend a lot of time in this book discussing various modules from the Python standard library, I have given a lot of web addresses (mostly in footnotes) to various parts of the documentation. The links all go to the Python 2 documentation, but you can easily get to the corresponding page for other versions by using the drop down menu in the top left of the page.

Example files

You can download a copy of the example files from here:

`http://pythonforbiologists.com/index.php/exercise-files/`

Save and extract the files into a folder wherever you like. The example files are separated by chapter. It should be possible to run most of them without modification. However, some require you to install modules that are not part of the Python standard library, and some (particularly those in the user interface folder) expect to be run with command line arguments. If in doubt, refer to the text.

For readers of my previous books

Anyone who has read *Python for Biologists* or *Advanced Python for Biologists* will notice a couple of ways in which this book is different. Most notably, I have not included exercises at the end of each chapter as I have in previous books. This is simply because the material doesn't lend itself to small, self-contained programming exercises. Unlike in previous books, where each chapter is devoted to a specific part of the language, in this book each chapter is more concerned with giving an overview of a particular aspect of software development. If it's not clear at the end of a given chapter how you can apply the material to your own work, it's probably because you haven't encountered that particular problem yet.

Chapter 1:Introduction

Readers of my previous books may recognize some of the example programs; in this book I've often used existing examples as starting points for discussion. Rest assured that if you notice slight differences in solutions to familiar problems in this book, it's because I've changed the code to better illustrate the ideas we are exploring.

Working on the command line

In this book we will be looking not just at the Python language itself, but also at other tools that help us to write Python more effectively. Many of these tools run on the command line, so in order to demonstrate them we'll have to look at command lines and command line output. In the chapter on performance we will use command line tools to benchmark and profile our code; in the chapter on testing we will use command line tools to run our tests, and in the chapter on user interfaces we will build a command line interface for a program we have written.

If you're not used to running programs on the command line then these examples may be difficult to interpret at first, but hopefully they will seem more familiar the more you read. It's certainly worth getting comfortable with using the command line as it's the only way to run many of the tools we want to use when developing in Python.

Typography and formatting

A book like this has lots of special types of text – we'll need to look at examples of Python code and output, the contents of files, and technical terms. Take a minute to note the typographic conventions we'll be using.

In the main text of this book, **bold type** is used to emphasize important points and *italics* for technical terms and filenames. Where code is mixed in with normal text it's written in a `monospaced font like this` with a grey background. Occasionally there are footnotes[1] to provide additional information that is interesting to know but not crucial to understanding, or to give links to web pages.

Example Python code is highlighted with a solid border above and below, and the name of the matching example file is written just underneath the example to the right:

```
Some example code goes here
```
example.py

Not every bit of code has a matching example file – much of the time we'll be building up a Python program bit by bit, in which case there will be a single example file containing the finished version of the program. The example files are in separate folders, one for each chapter, to make them easy to find.

Sometimes it's useful to refer to a specific line of code inside an example. For this, we'll use numbered circles like this ❶:

```
a line of example code
another line of example code
this is the important line  ❶
here is another line
```

Example output (i.e. what we see on the screen when we run the code) is highlighted with a dotted border:

```
Some output goes here
```

---

[1] Like this.

Chapter 1:Introduction

Often we want to look at the code and the output it produces together. In these situations, you'll see a solid-bordered code block followed immediately by a dotted-bordered output block.

Other blocks of text (usually file contents or typed command lines) don't have any kind of border and look like this:

```
contents of a file
```

There are many points in this book where we'll be looking at the output of command line tools. For these sections, the command line (i.e. what we type) always starts with a dollar symbol (the usual command prompt on Linux and Mac machines) with the output of the program underneath like this:

```
$ this is what we type
this is the first line of output
this is the second line of output
```

Just remember that whenever you see a line starting with a dollar symbol, that is that line that we are typing into the terminal.

When showing command lines that involve Python programs that don't have matching example files I'll use the filename *example.py* as a place holder like this:

```
$ python example.py
```

Occasionally we'll need to look at an example of an interactive Python session. In these cases, I'll use the three greater-than symbols to represent the usual Python interactive prompt like this:

```
>>> 2 + 2
4
```

Often when looking at larger examples, or when looking at large amounts of output, we don't need to see the whole thing. In these cases, I'll use ellipses (...) to indicate that some text has been missed out. For Python code, I will generally also leave out `import` statements to save space, though they will always be present in the example files.

I have used UK English spelling throughout, which I hope will not prove distracting to readers in other parts of the world.

Names

In chapters for which it makes sense to do so, I have tried to be generous with example files. In particular, the chapters on testing and on building user interfaces both contain many different versions of essentially the same program. This results in many different files with very similar names, so take care when running or referring to example files that you're looking at the right one. Remember that the matching file name is generally written underneath each example in the text in bold type.

In a similar way, I have often reused examples between chapters in order to take advantage of the reader's familiarity with them, so be careful of example files with very similar names in different chapters.

I have tried to use meaningful biological examples throughout, but have occasionally had to use very generic examples of functions, variables etc. For these instances I have used the traditional abstract variable names `foo` and `bar`.

When referring to names of Python packages and modules I have treated them as code, so they appear in monospaced type with a grey background e.g. `line_profiler`.

Getting in touch

Learning to program is a difficult task, and my one goal in writing this book is to make it as easy and accessible as possible to develop your programming skills. So, if you find anything that is hard to understand, or you think may contain an error, please get in touch – just drop me an email at

```
martin@pythonforbiologists.com
```

and I promise to get back to you. If you find the book useful, then please also consider leaving an Amazon review to help other people find it.

2: Environments for developing in Python

Introduction

One of the reasons that Python is such a great first language is that the tools for creating code are so simple. You can open a new file in any text editor, save your code, and then run it with a single command. And the way that Python is designed – with things like dynamic types and significant indentation – mean that you can get quite a long way writing programs with this very simple tool chain.

Eventually, however, we get to the point where there can be benefits from using more dedicated tools. Although these additional tools make life more complicated, they can also make developing software significantly easier. In this chapter, we're going to look at a few different types of tools which can help with common development tasks.

The chapter is divided into three main sections. We'll start with an overview of the various options for actually writing code: text editors, integrated development environments, and a couple of of other possibilities that are particularly interesting to scientists. Next, we'll look at tools which help us manage Python versions, packages and dependencies. Some of these are part of Python; others are more general purpose. Finally, we'll discuss a class of tool that you might not have used before: debuggers.

What you actually write code in

When you first started learning Python, you probably did one of two things: either you wrote your Python code in a text editor which you already used, or you used an *Integrated Development Environment* (usually shortened to IDE). There are advantages and disadvantages to both these approaches, so let's examine them in turn.

Text editors

Text editors are general purpose tools for editing text files, and if you're doing computational work in biology then you probably use them all the time. As you'll know if you've been programming for a while, many of the files that we work with in biology and bioinformatics are in plain text format, so a text editor is the tool of choice for viewing and editing[1]:

- sequence data formats like **FASTA** and **FASTQ** files
- genomic interval data like **BED** files
- read mapping data like **SAM** files
- variant information data like **VCF** files
- tabular data in **coma separated** or **tab separated** format

As well as storing data in plain text format, we also store things like

- **configuration files** for analysis tools like assemblers and read mappers
- **command lines** that we've figured out
- output from analysis programs like **BLAST**
- scripts and code for other languages (like **Perl** and **bash**)

The fact that we use a text editor for all these non-programming tasks in bioinformatics is a strong argument for using it to write our Python code as well. We can often be more productive by becoming familiar with a single tool and tailoring it to our work flow. Conversely, if we have to switch

---

[1] Insert examples from your own field if you don't recognize any of these names!

between multiple programs – with their different keyboard shortcuts, menu layouts, and settings – that can slow us down. If you already spend a lot of time in a text editor, you should consider using it for programming as well (and making an effort to learn how to use it most effectively!)

When it comes to individual text editors, it's tricky to make general recommendations, because so much depends on specific circumstances. However, here are a few things to consider when choosing a text editor:

Firstly, note that word processing tools like *Microsoft Word* and *LibreOffice Writer*, and online tools like *Google Docs*, **don't** count as text editors and are **not** good choices for writing code. They're optimized for making text look good on a page and include all sorts of formatting that Python can't understand. Even if you figure out how to get a word processor to output plain text, you'll be missing useful tools that other text editors have.

Secondly, there are a few features that pretty much everyone finds useful when writing code in a text editor. **Syntax highlighting**, in which different parts of code are displayed in different colours, can make it easier to spot certain types of syntax errors. **Tab emulation**, which allows the text editor to insert spaces when you press the tab key, helps to avoid the dreaded `IndentationError`. A powerful **find/replace tool** which supports **regular expressions** can be very useful for tidying up code and input files. Finally, the ability to **customize fonts** is surprisingly useful[1]; when programming, we want to see as many lines of code as clearly as possible (particularly important on small laptop screens).

Thirdly, consider whether you need a text editor that can run on a command line. More and more bioinformatics work is being carried out on

---

1   A particular quirk of Python is that we often type two underscores (as in names like `__future__` and `__init__`), so make sure whichever font you pick allows you to see the spaces between them – many otherwise good programming fonts don't. The code examples in this book are written in *Source Code Pro*, which is freely available.

Chapter 2:Environments for developing in Python

remote servers, and with the increasing interest in cloud computing that's likely to be even more true in the future. Although command line text editors can take a bit of getting used to, they generally work much more smoothly than graphical editors when working over a remote connection. Even if you only occasionally work on the command line, it's worth learning the basics of one of the simpler command line text editors.

Fourthly, some of the more sophisticated text editors have plugin systems which allows features to be added to them. These plugins often include features that are more commonly found in IDEs (some of which are described in the next section), so a text editor equipped with relevant plugins can sometimes offer a very nice development experience.

With these points out of the way, let's look at some specific recommendations.

If you want to try a basic command line editor, take a look at **nano.** The **nano** text editor is very simple, and has the additional bonus that it's already installed on most Linux and Mac machines. Despite being a very lightweight program, it has syntax highlighting (on most systems), tab emulation, and regular expression searching.

If you're looking for a simple graphical text editor, then the options depend on your operating system. If you use Windows, take a look at **Notepad++**[1]; if you use a Mac, take a look at **TextWrangler**[2], and if you're on Linux take a look at **Gedit**[3]. All three have the features we discussed above, plus many other useful tools.

---

1 https://notepad-plus-plus.org/
2 http://www.barebones.com/products/textwrangler/
3 https://wiki.gnome.org/Apps/Gedit

If you want to master a more complicated and capable command line text editor, then the two main options are **Vim**[1] and **Emacs**[2]. Both of these are mature, well established text editors with a wealth of settings and plugins – including many specifically designed to help you write Python code – to choose from.

Perhaps the best overall recommendation I can make for an advanced text editor is **Sublime Text**[3]. Unlike all of the other tools mentioned, it's not free, but it is an extremely powerful and fast graphical text editor which is designed for coding and which has a large ecosystem of plugins and extensions. It runs on OSX, Windows and Linux, so it's also a good choice if you regularly have to work on more than one operating system.

In the same category as Sublime Text is **Atom**[4], another text editor intended for code. It hasn't been in development as long as the others mentioned here, but is progressing rapidly and is well worth keeping an eye on.

There are, of course, thousands of other text editors out there, and if you already have a favourite which suits your needs, then it's fine to stick with it. Don't, however, fall into the common trap of confusing short-term and long-term productivity: switching to a text editor (or any tool) that you're not used to will always be awkward at first, but may pay off in the long term as you get more familiar with it.

Integrated development environments

If you take a text editor and add programming-specific tools, you get an *integrated development environment* or *IDE*. The word *integrated* in the name

---

[1] http://www.vim.org/
[2] https://www.gnu.org/software/emacs/
[3] http://www.sublimetext.com/
[4] https://atom.io/

Chapter 2:Environments for developing in Python

just means that all of the tools you use for software development are in one place. An IDE allows you to edit code, with all of the conveniences (like syntax highlighting) we've already discussed, but it also lets you do other things without having to switch to a separate program. For Python, these things include:

- run your code, or selected regions of code
- evaluate Python expressions in an interactive terminal
- run automated tests on your code[1] and view the results
- profile your code and view the results[2]
- debug your code using a graphical interface[3]
- refactor code (making it easy to do things like rename all references to a variable, or turn a chunk of code into a function)
- reformat your code (i.e. add spaces and newlines) to make it look pretty
- quickly move around in your code (for example, jump from a function call to the function definition)

As the name suggests, the value of an IDE lies in the integration: there are tools available for all these tasks already, but having them all in a single program can greatly speed up development.

Because of the way that Python is designed, some features that are present in IDEs for other languages are either not needed, or not present. For example, there's very little so-called "boilerplate" code[4] in Python, so we

---

[1] See the chapter on testing for an overview of why this is useful...
[2] ... and the chapter on profiling ...
[3] ... and the section on debugging at the end of this chapter.
[4] Boilerplate just means identical blocks of code that we need to include in our program many times.

generally don't need features for code generation. And because Python is dynamically typed, some types of refactoring are impossible. This goes some way toward explaining why IDEs are not as widespread in Python as in some other languages[1].

As you can probably gather from looking at the list of features, IDEs are most useful when dealing with large software projects. Larger projects tend to be the ones where we need to use testing and profiling, and in which navigating and refactoring across many files is the most difficult.

Learning to use an IDE effectively is a big time commitment, so if your projects are generally small and self contained then you might want to avoid them. However, it's perfectly possible to start using an IDE and only use the features you use – just treat it like a fancy text editor, and pick up the advanced features later on if you need them.

Just like text editors, there are many Python IDEs available, so we can only look at a few....

IDLE

We'll start with **IDLE** as it's the tool that you're most likely to have encountered before. It's often distributed along with Python, so if you have Python installed you probably also have IDLE. If you want to get a feeling for how developing in an IDE is different from developing using a text editor and command line, just launch IDLE and try it out for a few minutes.

As IDEs go, IDLE is a very basic one (by design; it's aimed at beginners). It has a text editor window and an interactive shell window and allows you to write and run Python code with minimal fuss. It has an interactive debugger, but no testing, profiling or refactoring tools. The user interface

---

[1] For example, it's a good bet that 99% of Java programmers are using an IDE, simply because the language lends itself to that type of tool.

is pretty dated, and most people that start with IDLE eventually move on to something more sophisticated. Because it requires zero set up, it's often used for teaching.

PyCharm

At the other end of the IDE spectrum from IDLE we find **PyCharm**[1]. It's a massively configurable program with just about every feature you could think of – far too many to list here. There are various versions, both free and paid. If you download and try it, you'll probably find it quite overwhelming if you've not used this kind of tool before, but there are some high quality tutorials available on the website[2] to help you get started.

Because of its many features, PyCharm is demanding of both processing power and memory, so if you do your coding on a low end computer or a laptop, you might want to give this one a miss.

Spyder

Here's an IDE of particular interest to us: **Spyder** is a programming environment that's designed specifically for scientific programming. To that end, it integrates with many of the libraries that are commonly used in scientific programming[3]. It lets you refer quickly to the documentation for classes and functions in commonly used libraries, and has some very nice features for data exploration – you can plot charts and other graphics directly in the output, and there are graphical editors for things like dicts and NumPy objects.

---

1   http://www.jetbrains.com/pycharm/
2   https://blog.jetbrains.com/pycharm/2016/01/introducing-getting-started-with-pycharm-video-tutorials/
3   Including NumPy, SciPy, Matplotlib and iPython.

IPython and Jupyter

The final tool that we're going to look at in terms of actually writing code is a tricky one to describe. It's like a combination of a note taking application, a text editor with special Python features, and an advanced interactive Python shell. Although this sounds like a confusing mess, iPython[1] is an incredible tool for scientists and is rapidly becoming the standard for exploratory programming and data analysis.

First, some history: originally **iPython** was developed as an advanced version of Python's interactive shell (i.e. what you get if you type `python` at the command line with no arguments). It behaved just like the regular shell, in that you could type in Python commands to be executed, but had some extra features like autocompletion and built in timing tools.

Later on, two massively important features were added: the ability to display graphics (especially charts) in the output, and a user interface that runs in a web browser (rather than the command line) and allows us to mix blocks of code with blocks of text. This browser based interface was so good that people started hacking it to work with other programming languages, and eventually the interface was split off as a separate project called **Jupyter**.

The reason that **iPython/Jupyter** is so useful is the ability to mix documentation, Python code, and graphical output in a single document. This makes it ideal for exploring a dataset, particularly in combination with data manipulation libraries like `pandas` and charting libraries like `matplotlib`. It's often referred to as the bioinformatics equivalent of the lab notebook: keeping your data, notes and output all in one place is tremendously helpful for organization.

---

1 http://ipython.org/

It's also becoming rapidly more popular as a way to display or communicate results. It's trivial to make a notebook publicly viewable, and a finished notebook can act like an interactive tutorial, where the user can edit and re-run the code.

If you ever use Python as a way to explore a dataset, or to investigate different ways of solving a problem, I strongly recommend you check out iPython.

Managing Python and packages

The problem of how to install a new package in Python is now pretty easily solved from the user's point of view: nearly everything can be done with the `pip` command[1]. There comes a point in every programmer's life, however, when they run into a classic dilemma: two different projects that require two different versions of the same package. This is a problem that can't be solved by any combination of installing or upgrading packages; what's needed is some way to have multiple different Python environments on the same computer.

Note: in the following description of environment managers, I'll show the commands for working on Linux and Mac computers. Things will look a bit different on Windows; follow the links to documentation for the individual projects to find out more.

The `virtualenv` tool[2] handles the job of managing multiple different Python environments. We call these *virtual environments*: a virtual environment is effectively a copy Python plus installed packages that's

---

[1] For an overview of the packaging process from the developer's point of view, take a look at the chapter on packaging.
[2] http://virtualenv.readthedocs.org/en/latest/index.html

isolated from every other copy. It's this isolation that allows multiple different versions of the same package to coexist happily on a single computer.

`virtualenv` is designed around the assumption that each virtual environment lives in its own folder. After installing `virtualenv` by running

```
$ sudo pip install virtualenv
```

most of what we need requires only three different commands. To create a new virtual environment, we run

```
$ virtualenv foo
```

which will create the folder *foo* and place a copy of the Python interpreter and *pip* inside it. To start using that virtual environment, we run the `activate` script inside that folder:

```
$ source foo/bin/activate
```

From now on, when we install packages they'll be installed into the *foo* virtual environment rather than the system one. To stop using this virtual environment, we run

```
$ deactivate
```

The `virtualenv` model works well for many tasks, but there are some circumstances where it becomes awkward. If we create a lot of new virtual environments for different projects, we'll end up with lots of `virtualenv` folders scattered around the file system, and every time we want to activate one, we have to remember its path.

It's also difficult to reuse the same virtual environment for multiple different projects, which is something we often want to do for data analysis. We might want to have a single virtual environment with all our

Chapter 2:Environments for developing in Python

data analysis packages – `pandas`, `numpy`, `matplotlib`, etc. – and use it to work on many different datasets.

Additionally, from an organizational point of view, it's not great to have virtual environment folders mixed in with folders containing data and results. It's especially annoying to use `virtualenv` with a shared filesystem, or a cloud service like *Dropbox* or *Google Drive*, since as soon as you create a new `virtualenv` folder it will start syncing.

The `virtualenvwrapper` package[1], as the name suggests, is a package that makes it easier to work with `virtualenv` environments in two important respects: it keeps all your virtual environments in one place, and it provides a convenient set of commands for working with them.

The set up for `virtualenvwrapper` is a bit more involved; we install it just like any other package:

```
$ pip install virtualenvwrapper
```

but we then have to add two lines to our shell profile (normally *~/.bash_profile* or *~/.bashrc*):

```
export WORKON_HOME=$HOME/.virtualenvs
source /usr/local/bin/virtualenvwrapper.sh
```

The first line tells `virtualenvwrapper` where we want to store our virtual environments. The second line makes the special `virtualenvwrapper` commands available (Windows users should ignore these instructions and go directly to the `virtualenvwrapper-win` project[2]).

Just like with `virtualenv`, when working with `virtualenvwrapper` the three main things we need to know is how to create virtual environments,

---

1   http://virtualenvwrapper.readthedocs.io/en/latest/
2   https://pypi.python.org/pypi/virtualenvwrapper-win

activate them, and deactivate them. To create a new virtual environment we run `mkvirtualenv` and give the new environment a name:

```
$ mkvirtualenv foo
```

Note that we don't have to worry about where we are in the filesystem as the virtual environment is going to be stored in whatever location we chose during set up. To start using a given environment we use the `workon` command:

```
$ workon foo
```

A couple of nice touches are that we don't have to run `workon` when we create a new environment – we start working on it automatically – and that we can use `workon` to switch directly from one environment to another.

To stop working on an environment and go back to the system default, we use `deactivate` just as before.

In general, I recommend `virtualenvwrapper` over `virtualenv`. The interface is easier to use, and it removes the annoyances associated with storing virtual environments in the filesystem.

Once we are used to the idea of virtual environments, it becomes clear that they solve a few other problems as well. If we don't have permissions to install packages in the system Python, we can install and use them in a virtual environment. If we want to test a piece of code under multiple different versions of a package, we can just create a virtual environment for each version that we're interested in. To install a specific version of a package, specify it in the `pip` command:

```
$ pip install mypackage=1.2.3
```

We can even test a piece of code under different versions of Python if we have them installed. Running `mkvirtualenv` with the -p option:

Chapter 2: Environments for developing in Python

```
$ mkvirtualenv foo_old_python -p /path/to/python/python2.3
```

will set the virtual environment to use a specific Python interpreter. This is very handy since when you're working in that virtual environment, running Python will call the version of Python that you specified:

```
$ workon foo_old_python
$ python
Python 2.3.0 ...
```

Another scenario in which virtual environments come in very handy is when developing packages of our own[1]. When preparing a package for distribution, we need to figure out the dependencies and write installation instructions. Creating a new, clean virtual environment is a tremendous help when doing this, as it allows us to easily simulate the environment of an end user installing our package for the first time. And once we've tested the installation process, being able to remove the virtual environment with a single command makes it easy to stay organized.

Containers

We finish this section with a couple of notes on tools which take the idea of a virtual environment even further. So far, we've seen that a virtual environment consists of a collection of specific Python packages (and interpreter), and that when we have multiple virtual environments on the same machine they are completely isolated from one another.

What if we wanted to do the same thing but with collections of programs, rather than just Python packages? This idea is called *containerization*, and there are several tools which implement it, the most popular currently being *Docker*[2]. The idea behind containers is that you package a piece of software (for readers of this book, probably a Python program that you

---

1   See the chapter on organizing and sharing code for an overview of package development in Python.
2   https://www.docker.com/

have written) with all its dependencies (other software tools and datasets which it requires to run) into one unit, which can then be distributed and installed easily.

Containers have some things in common with virtual environments: they both allow us to create multiple computing environments on a single computer which are completely isolated from one another. However, containers are different from virtual environments in two important respects. Firstly, they can contain any type of software and data, unlike virtual environments which can only contain Python packages. Secondly, they are explicitly designed to be **distributed** – tools like Docker make it easy to install a container (i.e. a piece of software plus all of its dependencies) on multiple computers. So containers really solve two problems: how to allow multiple bits of software to coexist on the same computer without interfering with each other, and how to distribute a complete computing environment.

A discussion of how to actually use containers is well beyond the scope of this book. If you think containers might be useful – and they are rapidly becoming a key tool in the area of reproducible science – the best place to start reading is probably the Docker documentation[1].

Virtual machines

The logical conclusion to thinking about multiple computing environments is to imagine running multiple different operating systems on a single computer. The term for this is a *virtual machine*, and historically, virtual machines have been used to address many of the same problems as containers and virtual environments. Whereas a virtual environment contains a collection of Python packages, and a container

---

1   https://docs.docker.com/engine/userguide/

contains a collection of programs, a virtual machine contains a complete operating system together with it's programs and data.

Like containers, virtual machines allow us to run multiple different computing environments on a single computer. Because they contain complete operating systems, virtual machines are an extremely flexible – we can use them, for example to run a dozen different versions of Windows, or many different distributions of Linux. This makes them the tool of choice for testing software on multiple operating systems, or for keeping an old version of an operating system running without having to dedicate a computer to the task.

Also like containers, virtual machines can be used to distribute a piece of software (e.g. a Python program) along with its dependencies, by creating a *virtual disk image* or a *virtual appliance*. In many cases, however, this approach is excessive, since we end up distributing a complete operating system whose size dwarfs that of the actual application we want to run.

If you want to try using virtual machines in your work, the easiest way to get started is with a tool called **VirtualBox**[1].

Working in a debugger

For the last section in this chapter we're going to look at a class of tools – debuggers – that are not necessary for software development, but are very useful.

To see why we need debuggers in the first place, we'll start with a tiny example. Imagine we want to write a piece of code that takes a DNA sequence and calculates the complement. We will start with a simple idea:

---

1   https://www.virtualbox.org/

first replace all **A** bases with **T**, then all **C** with **G**, then **G** with **C** and **T** with **A**[1].

```
dna = "ATGCGTGATGC"

dna = dna.replace("A", "T")
dna = dna.replace("C", "G")
dna = dna.replace("G", "C")
dna = dna.replace("T", "A")

print(dna)
```

complement.py

Running this code[2] gives an output that certainly looks like a DNA sequence:

```
AACCCACAACC
```

but just by glancing at it we can see that something is wrong. Our input sequence contained all four bases, but the output contains just **C** and **A**.

Let's see if we can figure out what's happening by looking at the sequence one base at a time[3]. The first base of the input sequence is **A**, therefore the first base of the output sequence should be its complement **T**, but we can see from the output that the first base is unchanged. This suggests an explanation: maybe the replacements simply aren't working and the sequence is being printed unchanged.

However, when we look at the second base, we can see that this explanation can't be right, because the second base has been correctly changed from **T** to **A**. Perhaps we have accidentally replaced all the bases

---

1   There are many better ways to do it, but this way makes a good example.
2   If you haven't already downloaded the example files, now would be a good time – go to http://pythonforbiologists.com/index.php/exercise-files/
3   If you gave already figured out what's happening, pretend you haven't and just follow the logic.

Chapter 2: Environments for developing in Python

with **A**? No, that's not true either, because the third base has been correctly changed from **G** to **C**.

It seems unlikely that we can figure out what's going on just by looking at the input and output sequences. To find the source of the error we're going to need to look at the intermediate steps as well. Our next move will probably be something like this:

```
dna = "ATGCGTGATGC"
print("original:           " + dna)

dna = dna.replace("A", "T")
print("first replacement:  " + dna)

dna = dna.replace("C", "G")
print("second replacement: " + dna)

dna = dna.replace("G", "C")
print("third replacement:  " + dna)

dna = dna.replace("T", "A")
print("fourth replacement: " + dna)
```

complement_with_print.py

This approach works well enough; the output allows us to see what's happening:

```
original:            ATGCGTGATGC
first replacement:   TTGCGTGTTGC
second replacement:  TTGGGTGTTGG
third replacement:   TTCCCTCTTCC
fourth replacement:  AACCCACAACC
```

If we just follow the fate of the first base, we can see that in the first replacement it gets changed from **A** to **T**, but then in the fourth replacement it gets changed from **T** back to **A**. In other words, by the time we get to the fourth replacement we have no way of knowing which **T** bases were **T** in the original sequence, and which ones were originally **A**. The same logic applies to **G** and **C**, which explains why we only see **A** and **C** in the final output.

Once we've seen the error there are many different ways to fix it. The simplest is probably to do the replacement in lower case, then convert the sequence back to upper case once the replacements have been made (this works because the `replace()` method is case sensitive):

```
dna = "ATGCGTGATGC"
print("original:            " + dna)

dna = dna.replace("A", "t")
print("first replacement:   " + dna)

...

dna = dna.upper()
print("finally:             " + dna)
```

complement_fixed.py

In this case, the "print everything" approach worked, because the code was very short and the problem obvious once we looked at the output. But the process of solving the problem in this way has several drawbacks.

Firstly it involved a lot of editing: we had to insert `print()` statements after every statement in the original code – making it twice as long – and then look through the output. Once we found the problem and fixed it, we would then have to go back to the code and delete or comment out all of the `print()` statements. For larger, more complex programs, this approach simply wouldn't be feasible.

Secondly, because we didn't initially know the source of the problem we had no choice but to print after every single step in the code. For a very small program like this one that's not too bad, but for a larger program the amount of printed output might be very large and difficult to sort through. The situation would be even worse for a program that produced output while it was normally running – in that case, our debugging output would be mixed up with the normal output of the program and it would be even harder to interpret.

Finally, the approach that we took to fixing the problem is not very interactive. We add some `print()` statements, run the program, look at the output, edit the code, run the program again, look at the output again, etc. A more powerful approach would allow us to change the variables and the code interactively while the program is running.

In this section we'll look at a type of tool that helps to address all three points: a *debugger*. A debugger allows us to interactively examine and change code while it's running, and is a much better way of tracking down errors than the "print everything" approach. There are many debuggers available for Python but they all share a bunch of basic concepts, so we'll concentrate mainly on the one that's part of the standard library and only consider others at the end.

A couple of quick notes before we dive in. As with many of the tools in this book, coming up with useful examples for debugging is tricky. Debugging tools are most useful when working with long, complicated programs, but examples need to be short and simple so that we can easily understand them. For most of the examples in this section, we'll start with a program that contains a bug or error, and use a debugger to fix them. But because the examples are short and simple, you might find that you can easily spot the error by looking at the code. If this happens, just pretend you didn't see it and read on – in the real world, you'll working on more complicated programs in which it will be much harder to spot bugs manually.

Chapter 2:Environments for developing in Python

Similarly, you may be able to think of better ways to write most of the example program that we'll examine in this section – perhaps even ways that would prevent the errors from occurring in the first place! Again, if this happens just read on; the examples have been deliberately written to illustrate common errors.

Looking at variables

The standard Python debugger is called `pdb` and lives in a module of the same name. Let's go back to our original, faulty program:

```
dna = "ATGCGTGATGC"

dna = dna.replace("A", "T")
dna = dna.replace("C", "G")
dna = dna.replace("G", "C")
dna = dna.replace("T", "A")

print(dna)
```
complement.py

and analyse it with a debugger rather than with `print()` statements. To do this, we import the `pdb` module then call the `set_trace()` function at the point where we want to start debugging the program:

```
import pdb

dna = "ATGCGTGATGC"
pdb.set_trace()
dna = dna.replace("A", "T")
dna = dna.replace("C", "G")
dna = dna.replace("G", "C")
dna = dna.replace("T", "A")

print(dna)
```
complement_pdb.py

Chapter 2:Environments for developing in Python

Let's see what happens when we run the program now:

```
$ python complement_pdb.py
> complement_pdb.py(5)<module>()
-> dna = dna.replace("A", "T")
(Pdb)
```

On the first line of output we have the command line that we typed to run our program. The next line tells us the name of the file (*complement_pdb.py*) and the line number that is about to execute (5)[1]. The next line, which starts with an arrow -> shows the actual code on that line. Finally, we have the pdb prompt (Pdb) which is waiting for an instruction from us.

There are two important things to recognize here. The first is that the program is actually in the middle of running, and has effectively paused on the line where we called `set_trace()`. That's why we don't yet see the output sequence printed; the program has only run for the first few lines and hasn't finished yet. The second is that the program is now running interactively under the debugger – it won't continue running until we tell it to.

We'll get started with pdb by learning a few commands. To view the code we can use the l command (short for **list**). If we type l at the pdb prompt and press enter, we'll see the code surrounding the current line with an arrow pointing to the current line:

---

[1] This will look slightly different if you run it on your system, as it depends on the path to the Python file.

```
(Pdb) l
  1      import pdb
  2
  3      dna = "ATGCGTGATGC"
  4      pdb.set_trace()
  5  ->  dna = dna.replace("A", "T")
  6      dna = dna.replace("C", "G")
  7      dna = dna.replace("G", "C")
  8      dna = dna.replace("T", "A")
  9
 10      print(dna)
[EOF]
```

Because our program is so short, this command actually shows us the whole program, but for a longer one it would just show the bits immediately before and after the current line.

To view the content of variables just like we were previously doing with our `print()` statements we can use the p command (short for print). We type p followed by the variable we want to examine. In this program there's only one variable, dna:

```
(Pdb) p dna
'ATGCGTGATGC'
```

Notice that the output of this command is not exactly the same as we got from our `print()` statements: this is Python's own internal representation of the value, so it includes the quotes surrounding the string.

Looking carefully at the output we can see that dna is exactly the same as it was at the start of the program. In other words, the current line (i.e. the one that replaces **A** with **T**) has not yet been executed. This is important to keep in mind when using a debugger: whenever we refer to the current line we mean the one that is about to be executed, **not** the one that has just been executed.

Chapter 2:Environments for developing in Python

Let's go ahead and tell pdb to execute the first replacement. To do so, we use the n command (short for next). When we type n and press enter, pdb executes the current line and then displays the current file, line number, and current line just as it did when we first started running the program:

```
(Pdb) n
> complement_pdb.py(6)<module>()
-> dna = dna.replace("C", "G")
```

Now that the first replacement has been carried out, we can take a look at the dna variable again:

```
(Pdb) p dna
'TTGCGTGTTGC'
```

and confirm that it has been changed. Hopefully at this point we will notice the problem; if not, we can simply keep running the program with the n command and viewing the DNA sequence with the p command until we get to the end:

```
(Pdb) n
> complement_pdb.py(7)<module>()
-> dna = dna.replace("G", "C")
(Pdb) p dna
'TTGGGTGTTGG'
(Pdb) n
> complement_pdb.py(8)<module>()
-> dna = dna.replace("T", "A")
(Pdb) p dna
'TTCCCTCTTCC'
(Pdb) n
> complement_pdb.py(10)<module>()
-> print(dna)
(Pdb) p dna
'AACCCACAACC'
```

Although at first this approach to debugging seems more complicated than simply using `print()` statements, it's better in several ways. Unlike the "print everything" approach, it required only minimal changes to the code. If, after having fixed the problem, we want to restore the code to running normally, all we have to do is delete or comment out the `pdb.set_trace()` line.

It's also much easier (once we get used to the `pdb` interface) to interpret the values of the `dna` variable, even though we're looking at exactly the same data. With the `print()` statement approach we just get a collection of output lines, whereas with `pdb` we can see the values of the `dna` variable in context with the lines of code that are changing it.

Controlling the debugger

To explore the features of `pdb` in more detail, let's switch to a more complicated example. Here's a piece of code that calculates the average AT content of a list of DNA sequences[1]:

```
sequences = [
'ATCGTAGTCGA',
'ATCGTTAGCT',
'ATCGTAGCGTGTAC'
]

for dna in sequences:
    total_at = 0
    for base in dna:
        if base == 'A' or base == 'T':
            total_at = total_at + 1

total_length = sum(map(len, sequences))

print("average AT content: " + str(total_at/total_length))
```

`at_content.py`

For each DNA sequence we examine each base in turn and if it's **A** or **T** we add it to a total count. After processing all the sequences we find the total number of bases by summing the lengths of the sequences, then divide the

---

1   As before, if you spot the flaw in this code right away then pretend you don't :-)

Chapter 2:Environments for developing in Python

total AT count by the length to get the result. The output looks kind of plausible:

```
average AT content: 0.2
```

until you look closely at the sequences and notice that they look to be about equally composed of all four bases, which would make an AT content of 0.2 far too low.

Let's see if we can figure out what's happening by using the "print everything" approach. Unlike our first example, where we required multiple `print()` statements, with this example we just need a single one inside the loop:

```
sequences = [...]

for dna in sequences:
    total_at = 0
    for base in dna:
        if base == 'A' or base == 'T':
            total_at = total_at + 1
        print(total_at)
...
```

at_content_with_print.py

Unfortunately, the resulting output is not very useful:

```
1
2
2
2
3
4
4
5
5
5
6
1
2
2
2
3
...
```

We get a string of numbers which tells us that the `total_at` variable is sometimes increasing, sometimes decreasing, and sometimes staying the same, but there's no way to correlate it with what's going on in the code.

Let's try firing up the debugger instead. We'll put the `pdb.set_trace()` function call on the same line that we had the `print()` statement:

```
sequences = [...]

for dna in sequences:
    total_at = 0
    for base in dna:
        if base == 'A' or base == 'T':
            total_at = total_at + 1
        pdb.set_trace()
...
```

at_content_pdb.py

Notice what happens when we run the program and enter the `pdb` prompt:

Chapter 2:Environments for developing in Python

```
$ python at_content_pdb.py
> at_content_pdb.py(12)<module>()
-> for base in dna:
(Pdb)
```

Because the `pdb.set_trace()` line is at the end of the `for` loop, when we enter the debugger the current line (i.e. the one we're about to execute) is the start of the next iteration of the loop. Running the `l` command makes it a bit clearer:

```
(Pdb) l
  7         'ATCGTAGCGTGTAC'
  8     ]
  9
 10     for dna in sequences:
 11         total_at = 0
 12  -> for base in dna:
 13             if base == 'A' or base == 'T':
 14                 total_at = total_at + 1
 15         pdb.set_trace()
 16
```

Notice that, unlike our first example, this one is long enough that we can't see the start or end of the code, just the bit that is currently running. We can use the `p` command to examine the state of the `total_at` variable:

```
(Pdb) p total_at
1
```

and so far everything looks fine: we have counted the first base of the first sequence, which is **A**, so the count is one. One of the nice things about using the debugger is that we can keep track of multiple variables at the same time using the `p` command – let's print the values of the `total_at` variable, the `base` variable, and the `dna` variable:

```
(Pdb) p total_at, base, dna
(1, 'A', 'ATCGTAGTCGA')
```

Chapter 2:Environments for developing in Python

Next, what we'd like to do is run the program while keeping track of these three variables for each iteration of the loop. If we try to use the n command as we did before, however, we run into a problem:

```
(Pdb) n
> at_content_pdb.py(13)<module>()
-> if base == 'A' or base == 'T':
```

The n command only executes the next line – in other words, it moves us on to the first line inside the loop. That's not what we want: we want to run the whole loop and then stop and check the variables. We could simply run the n command multiple times, but that will quickly get tedious. Instead, we'll run the c command (short for continue) which will allow the program to continue running until it hits the next iteration of the `pdb.set_trace()` line:

```
(Pdb) c
> at_content_pdb.py(12)<module>()
-> for base in dna:
```

This puts us back at the same place in the code we were before – the start of the loop – but after the next complete iteration. We can check this by running our p command again:

```
(Pdb) p total_at, base, dna
(2, 'T', 'ATCGTAGTCGA')
```

and seeing that we have now counted the first two bases, and that the last base we examined was **T** (the second base of the first sequence). Rather than typing out this p command each time we want to run it, we can just take advantage of the pdb history and press the up arrow to repeat previous commands.

We'll continue to run the loop and monitor the variables by alternating the c command with the p command until we see something interesting:

Chapter 2:Environments for developing in Python

```
(Pdb) c
> at_content_pdb.py(12)<module>()
-> for base in dna:
(Pdb) p total_at, base, dna
(2, 'G', 'ATCGTAGTCGA')

...

(Pdb) p total_at, base, dna
(6, 'A', 'ATCGTAGTCGA')  ❶
(Pdb) c ❷
> at_content_pdb.py(12)<module>()
-> for base in dna:
(Pdb) p total_at, base, dna  ❸
(1, 'A', 'ATCGTTAGCT')
```

From the last few lines in this session after the ellipses, we can see what's going on. Initially we are at the end of the first DNA sequence: we have just counted the last base, which is an A, and the total count is 6❶. Everything looks fine so far. We then run the `c` command❷, which moves us on to the first base of the second sequence. When we examine the variables again❸, we see that – as expected – the `dna` variable has changed, but also that – unexpectedly – the `total_at` variable has gone down to one. Running the `l` command lets us see the code surrounding the place where the problem occurs:

```
(Pdb) l
  7         'ATCGTAGCGTGTAC'
  8     ]
  9
 10     for dna in sequences:
 11         total_at = 0
 12  -> for base in dna:
 13             if base == 'A' or base == 'T':
 14                 total_at = total_at + 1
 15         pdb.set_trace()
 16
```

and on the line just before the inner `for` loop we see the line that's causing the error. We are resetting the `total_at` variable back to zero at the start of each sequence – an easy mistake to make! Instead, we should be creating it once at the start of the program. Making the fix:

```
sequences = [ ... ]
total_at = 0

for dna in sequences:
    for base in dna:
        ...

total_length = sum(map(len, sequences))

print("average AT content: " + str(total_at/total_length))
```

at_content_fixed.py

causes the program to give the right answer:

```
average AT content: 0.542857142857
```

Running code and changing variables

So far, we have been using the debugger simply to control the execution of a program and to monitor the variables that we're interested in. There's a lot more we can do, however – when typing at the pdb prompt we are actually interacting with a complete Python environment. This means that we can execute arbitrary code that's not in our program, and even change the value of variables while the code is running.

As an example, let's look at a different way to calculate AT content:

```
dna = raw_input("Enter a DNA sequence:\n")
at = dna.count('A') + dna.count('T') / len(dna)
print("AT content is " + str(at))
```

at_content_input.py

Chapter 2:Environments for developing in Python

This code will get the user to type in a DNA sequence then print the AT content. We'll try running it with a very short DNA sequence – ATGC – where we know that the correct answer is 0.5:

```
$ python at_content_input.py
Enter a DNA sequence:
ATGC
AT content is 1.25
```

We might guess that the reason for the incorrect code is that one of the three numbers involved in the calculation – the A count, the T count, or the length – is wrong. Let's start the debugger just after we calculate the AT content:

```
import pdb

dna = raw_input("Enter a DNA sequence:\n")
at = dna.count('A') + dna.count('T') / len(dna)
pdb.set_trace()
print("AT content is " + str(at))
```

at_content_input_pdb.py

Now when we run the program it asks us for the DNA sequence before dropping us at the **pdb** prompt:

```
$ python at_content_input_pdb.py
Enter a DNA sequence:
ATGC
> at_content_input_pdb.py (5)<module>()
-> print("AT content is " + str(at))
(Pdb)
```

Because at this point in the program the AT content has been calculated, we can print it using the **p** command:

```
(Pdb) p at
1.25
```

Chapter 2:Environments for developing in Python

but that doesn't tell us anything we didn't already know. What we really want to examine are the three numbers used to calculate the AT content. However, because we calculated those numbers and used them immediately rather than storing them in variables, there's no variable that we can print. Instead, we have to evaluate the same expressions by simply typing them at the prompt:

```
(Pdb) dna.count('A')
1
(Pdb) dna.count('T')
1
(Pdb) len(dna)
4
```

Surprisingly, all these values look fine. Perhaps the problem is something to do with the calculation itself. Let's recreate it by simply typing it at the pdb prompt (one quirk of pdb under Python 2 is that there's no way to get automatic floating point division, so we have to make it explicit):

```
(Pdb) float(dna.count('A')) + float(dna.count('T')) / len(dna)
1.25
```

As expected, we get exactly the same (incorrect) value as we did before. Perhaps it is something to do with precedence; let's try using parentheses to make sure that the addition happens before the division:

```
(Pdb) (float(dna.count('A')) + float(dna.count('T'))) / len(dna)
0.5
```

Now we get the correct answer (remember that rather than typing the whole line out again we can just press the up arrow to go back in pdb's history, then edit the line and hit enter).

Finally, we would like to check that the output prints correctly. However, we know that the current value of at our program's memory is the incorrect one. Let's fix it by changing the value to use the correct

Chapter 2: Environments for developing in Python

calculation, then run the current line (which contains the `print()` statement) and look at the output:

```
(Pdb) at = (float(dna.count('A')) + float(dna.count('T'))) / len(dna)
(Pdb) n
AT content is 0.5
--Return--
```

Everything looks OK now, so we can now exit the debugger and make the changes to our program code. This was a trivial example – we could have very easily figured it out by looking more closely at the code, or by inserting a few `print()` statements. Alternatively, we could have run an interactive Python session:

```
$ python -i at_content_input.py
...
```

to experiment with the different numbers in the calculation. However, for more complicated problems the ability of `pdb` to evaluate arbitrary statements and to change variables while a program is running makes it very powerful.

Controlling program execution

So far, our options for controlling the flow of our debugging session have been rather limited. We can tell `pdb` to pause execution using `pdb.set_trace()`, and then at the `pdb` prompt we can either tell it to execute the next line or continue to the next `pdb.set_trace()` statement. To finish our look at `pdb`, we'll consider a few examples that requires some more sophisticated control.

Imagine we want to write a piece of code that takes a DNA sequence and produces a protein translation. We might start by defining a dict to store the genetic code: the keys will be codons and the values will be amino acid residues:

```
gencode = {
    'ATA':'I', 'ATC':'I', 'ATT':'I', 'ATG':'M',
    ...
    }
```

dna_translation.py

We'll also define a function to take a DNA sequence and split it into codons:

```
def split_dna(dna):
    codons = []
    for start in range(0,len(dna), 3):   ❶
        codons.append(dna[start:start+3])   ❷
    return codons
```

dna_translation.py

Inside the function, we iterate over the list of codon start position by using a range that goes from zero to the length of the DNA sequence in steps of 3❶. For each codon start position we add three to get the stop position and extract the substring between those two positions❷.

To carry out the actual translation:

```
dna = 'ATCGATCGGATCGAT'

protein = ""
for codon in split_dna(dna):   ❶
    aa = gencode.get(codon)   ❷
    protein = protein + aa   ❸
print(protein)
```

dna_translation.py

we call our `split_dna()` function then iterate over the returned list❶. For each codon we look up the corresponding amino acid from the dict❷ and add it to a growing protein string❸.

Chapter 2: Environments for developing in Python

Running the program with the test DNA sequence works fine and produces a short protein sequence:

```
IDRID
```

But running it with a longer one:

```
...
dna = 'GTTCACTTGGCCAAGCTATC'
...
```

causes an error:

```
$ python dna_translation.py
Traceback (most recent call last):
  File "dna_translation.py", line 29, in <module>
    aa = gencode[codon]
KeyError: 'TC'
```

To start tracking down the source of the error we'll use `pdb` as before, but rather than importing it and using `pdb.set_trace()` we'll load it on the command line:

```
$ python -m pdb dna_translation.py
> dna_translation.py(1)<module>()
-> gencode = {
(Pdb)
```

This is just another way of using `pdb`; it's roughly equivalent to importing it and adding `pdb.set_trace()` right at the start of the program, but doesn't require us to edit the code. Notice that the current line (indicated by an arrow ->) is the very first line of the program, where we start to define the genetic code dict.

Chapter 2:Environments for developing in Python

What we'd like to do first of all is to try running the `split_dna()` function on some test inputs to see how it behaves. However, if we look at the structure of the program, we can see that this is going to be awkward:

```
gencode = {
    'ATA':'I', 'ATC':'I', 'ATT':'I', 'ATG':'M',
    'ACA':'T', 'ACC':'T', 'ACG':'T', 'ACT':'T',
    'AAC':'N', 'AAT':'N', 'AAA':'K', 'AAG':'K',
    'AGC':'S', 'AGT':'S', 'AGA':'R', 'AGG':'R',
    'CTA':'L', 'CTC':'L', 'CTG':'L', 'CTT':'L',
    'CCA':'P', 'CCC':'P', 'CCG':'P', 'CCT':'P',
    'CAC':'H', 'CAT':'H', 'CAA':'Q', 'CAG':'Q',
    'CGA':'R', 'CGC':'R', 'CGG':'R', 'CGT':'R',
    'GTA':'V', 'GTC':'V', 'GTG':'V', 'GTT':'V',
    'GCA':'A', 'GCC':'A', 'GCG':'A', 'GCT':'A',
    'GAC':'D', 'GAT':'D', 'GAA':'E', 'GAG':'E',
    'GGA':'G', 'GGC':'G', 'GGG':'G', 'GGT':'G',
    'TCA':'S', 'TCC':'S', 'TCG':'S', 'TCT':'S',
    'TTC':'F', 'TTT':'F', 'TTA':'L', 'TTG':'L',
    'TAC':'Y', 'TAT':'Y', 'TAA':'_', 'TAG':'_',
    'TGC':'C', 'TGT':'C', 'TGA':'_', 'TGG':'W'}

def split_dna(dna):
    codons = []
    for start in range(0,len(dna), 3):
        codons.append(dna[start:start+3])
    return codons

# this is where we want to get to
```

We need to execute all the lines that define the dict, then all the lines that define the `split_dna()` function before we can start our tests. We don't have a `pdb.set_trace()` line, so we can't simply use the `c` (for continue) command as we did before, so we'll have to run the `n` (for next) command 24 times.

Alternatively, we could set a *breakpoint*. A breakpoint is just our way of telling `pdb` that we want to stop the code at a particular line: to create one, we use the `b` command and give the line number that we want to stop at – in this case, 25:

Chapter 2:Environments for developing in Python

```
(Pdb) b 25
Breakpoint 1 at debugging/dna_translation.py:25
```

You can see how pdb helpfully prints a message telling us that it's added a breakpoint. We can now use c for continue and pdb will run the program until it hits line 25 where the dna variable is defined:

```
(Pdb) c
> dna_translation.py(25)<module>()
-> dna = 'GTTCACTTGGCCAAGCTATC'
(Pdb)
```

Now we can experiment with running the split_dna() function on a few different inputs. With our original DNA sequence everything looks fine:

```
(Pdb) split_dna('ATCGATCGGATCGAT')
['ATC', 'GAT', 'CGG', 'ATC', 'GAT']
```

but with the DNA sequence that caused the error we can see what's going wrong:

```
(Pdb) split_dna('GTTCACTTGGCCAAGCTATC')
['GTT', 'CAC', 'TTG', 'GCC', 'AAG', 'CTA', 'TC']
```

Because the length of the sequence isn't an exact multiple of three, there is an incomplete codon at the end of the list, which doesn't appear in the genetic code dict and therefore causes a KeyError when we try to look it up.

Let's test this theory by executing the current line (which defines the troublesome DNA sequence), editing it to remove the last two bases, then allowing the program to finish running:

```
(Pdb) n
> dna_translation.py(27)<module>()
-> protein = ""
(Pdb) dna = 'GTTCACTTGGCCAAGCTA'
(Pdb) c
VHLAKL
```

As we can see from the final line of output, the sequence now translates without any error. This experiment proves that it was the length of the sequence, and not anything to do with the actual bases, that caused the error. To prevent this error from happening again, we can edit the `range()` argument to exclude any partial codons at the end of the sequence:

```
def split_dna(dna):
    codons = []
    for start in range(0,len(dna) - 2, 3):
        codons.append(dna[start:start+3])
    return codons
```

dna_translation_fixed.py

Debugging exceptions

Here's a more sophisticated version of our DNA translation program:

```
gencode = {
    'ATA':'I', 'ATC':'I', 'ATT':'I', 'ATG':'M',
    ...
}

def split_dna(dna):
    codons = []
    for start in range(0,len(dna) - 2, 3):
        codons.append(dna[start:start+3])
    return(codons)

def translate(dna):
    protein = ""
    for codon in split_dna(dna):
        aa = gencode.get(codon)
        protein = protein + aa
    return(protein)

for line in open("seqs.txt"):
    print(translate(line.rstrip("\n")))
```

Chapter 2:Environments for developing in Python

dna_translation_from_file.py

The code is the same, but now it's structured into two functions and has a loop that will translate all the DNA sequences in a file. Running the program produces a whole lot of valid output, followed by a crash:

```
GLSDA_VSLMALTRSWLCKNT_RLKFVARDRLPLQRGKIRSLGAAYSDQLVSGAPRINPIKRIQYDRLTYYTCG
QVSLT_S_WSLWVNQRAFQL__VYIMLAISHASYYQPTANNGPRSIVPLNRTWGCTS_IV_GCASKLSPSLCGY
RFAPRHLGPVLIHSCQNKISIGL_AG_PQNKIDMD_KRPTHTRLADRLSRTSPNLPWLLTLSILLGEW_ALSVM
RLRNCRRSVLGAGTVPPREEVR_GFE_GIQ_LLFLS_AVGPNRASKRNGR_PSRACSARCRGVSTREKHLPLKG
...
Traceback (most recent call last):
  File "dna_translation_from_file.py", line 33, in <module>
    print(translate(line.rstrip("\n")))
  File "dna_translation_from_file.py", line 29, in translate
    protein = protein + aa
TypeError: cannot concatenate 'str' and 'NoneType' objects
```

If we take a look at the *seqs.txt* input file, we can see straight away that this problem is going to be a bit tricky to track down – there are 1000 DNA sequences in the file, so examining them manually one by one to see if anything looks wrong would be very time consuming. Similarly, it's not really feasible to start the program running under the debugger, as we'd have to continue through hundreds of sequences before we get to the one that caused the problem.

Instead, we need to start the debugger at the point where the problem occurs. One option is to use a `try/except` block to start the debugger if there's an exception:

```
for line in open("seqs.txt"):
    try:
        print(translate(line.rstrip("\n")))
    except:
        pdb.set_trace()
```

dna_translation_from_file_try.py

Chapter 2:Environments for developing in Python

This works, and when we run the program again we get dropped into the `pdb` prompt following the exception:

```
$ python dna_translation_from_file_try.py
PLIRAKRCPPGRCDAYEFSAFWSLCCRYKG_KHAAF___HT_LTVLQSAQ_L_FLSNGEW_YCIRPGIGRYR
VKLNVVTGFSGFGDLHAAPELSLEFAAVHSASPEWLIQSRLLLRGRWMELHNDPYITMV_CVLLRTS_WFCV
...
> dna_translation_from_file_try.py(34)<module>()
-> for line in open("seqs.txt"):
```

which allows us to view the line that caused the crash:

```
(Pdb) p line
'ACCCCAACAGTGATAGCACCGCGCTTAGTTCGCTCCGAAAAGTTCTTGATCATGTAGAAATCTCGGGTGCTGG
GGGCGGGGCCGCTGGGCTACCTGAATGATTCAGTACTACCTCTCGCGAATTCGGTAGTCTCCCANTCAGTCCGT
CCCGGCTATATAGTATCTACATTCGATGAGTCCTATCGCGCGGAGCCAAAGGACGAGAGAACCGAAGGTGCACG
GTGATCGTTCGGTTGTGGTCCTACGCCTCCTGGCCATTTGTATGCTTATGATGTCCA\n'
(Pdb)
```

That's a good start, but still not very helpful – that's still too much data to examine manually. What we'd really like to be able to do is to examine the individual codon that caused the crash, but if we try to do so:

```
(Pdb) p codon
*** NameError: NameError("name 'codon' is not defined",)
```

we find that it's not defined at this point in the code, since its scope is limited to the `translate()` function.

To properly analyze this crash, we need to use the `pdb.post_mortem()` function:

```
for line in open("seqs.txt"):
    try:
        print(translate(line.rstrip("\n")))
    except:
        pdb.post_mortem()
```
---

dna_translation_from_file_postmortem.py

which will cause the debugger to start at the point where the exception is raised[1] (i.e. inside the `translate()` function) rather than where it is caught:

```
$ python dna_translation_from_file_postmortem.py
PLIRAKRCPPGRCDAYEFSAFWSLCCRYKG_KHAAF___HT_LTVLQSAQ_L_FLSNGEW_YCIRPGIGRYR
VKLNVVTGFSGFGDLHAAPELSLEFAAVHSASPEWLIQSRLLLRGRWMELHNDPYITMV_CVLLRTS_WFCV
...
> dna_translation_from_file_postmortem.py(31)translate()
-> protein = protein + aa
```

Notice how this time, we enter the code at line 31 rather than line 34, and that the next line is the one where we append the amino acid. We can now examine the amino acid that caused the problem:

```
(Pdb) p aa
None
```

It turns out that the `aa` variable, rather than holding a string representing an amino acid residue, held the value `None`. To figure out why this was the case, we can look at the codon:

```
(Pdb) p codon
'CAN'
```

and finally the mystery is solved: the codon contained an undetermined base, which meant that it wasn't in the dict, which caused `gencode.get(codon)` to return `None`, which caused an exception when we tried to append it to a string. Happily, the fix is straightforward: adding a default to the `get()` method:

---

[1] This is a simplification: pdb actually uses the traceback from the exception to figure out where to start debugging.

```
def translate(dna):
    protein = ""
    for codon in split_dna(dna):
        aa = gencode.get(codon, '*')
        protein = protein + aa
    return(protein)
```

dna_translation_from_file_fixed.py

allows all of the input sequences to be processed, with asterisks inserted to represent an unknown amino acid for any codon that contains an undetermined base.

Jumping in and out of functions

For the last example in this chapter, we'll revisit an idea from earlier: calculating AT content. Imagine we have written the following function:

```
def at_content(dna):
    a = dna.find("A")
    t = dna.find("T")
    at_content = (a + t) / len(dna)
    return at_content
```

at_content_function.py

We want to use it to calculate the AT content of a collection of sequences, but are worried that they might contain undetermined bases, so we write a function that will clean up the DNA sequences by removing any character that isn't a base:

```
def clean_dna(dna):
    result = ""
    for base in dna:
        if base.upper() in ['A', 'T', 'G', 'C']:
            result = result + base.upper()
    return result
```

Chapter 2:Environments for developing in Python

at_content_function.py

and we try out our two functions on a few test sequences:

```
seqs = [
    "actgtacgtacgtagctacg", # this sequence is in lower case
    "CGGCTGGTGTTAACGGCTAT",
    "ACTGTGANTGCTCGATGTGC", # this sequence contains an N
    "CGCNTCGTGCTA"          # so does this one
]

for dna in seqs:
    print("looking at sequence: " + dna)
    cleaned = clean_dna(dna)
    at = at_content(cleaned)
    print("at content is " + str(at))
```

at_content_function.py

We expect all the values to be between zero and one, but that's not the output we get:

```
looking at sequence: actgtacgtacgtagctacg
at content is 0.1
looking at sequence: CGGCTGGTGTTAACGGCTAT
at content is 0.75
looking at sequence: ACTGTGANTGCTCGATGTGC
at content is 0.105263157895
looking at sequence: CGCNTCGTGCTA
at content is 1.18181818182
```

When we encountered this error previously, it was because we had forgotten to put parentheses around the addition part of the calculation, but this time we included the parentheses from the start, so that can't be the problem.

To start tracking down the source of the error we'll start the debugger at the beginning of the loop so that we can follow what happens:

```
for dna in seqs:
    pdb.set_trace()
    print("looking at sequence: " + dna)
    ...
```

at_content_function_pdb.py

Running the program puts us at the `pdb` prompt before any output is printed:

```
$ python at_content_function_pdb.py
> at_content_function_pdb.py (27)<module>()
-> print("looking at sequence: " + dna)
(Pdb)
```

and we can now step through the body of the loop. We'll use the `n` command twice to move to the point where we have the cleaned sequence, then examine it:

```
(Pdb) n
looking at sequence: actgtacgtacgtagctacg
> at_content_function_pdb.py (28)<module>()
-> cleaned = clean_dna(dna)
(Pdb) n
> at_content_function_pdb.py (29)<module>()
-> at = at_content(cleaned)
(Pdb) p cleaned
'ACTGTACGTACGTAGCTACG'
```

That looks fine, so the problem must lie in the code that calculates the AT content. Ideally we would like to be able to examine the variables `a` and `t` which hold the counts, but look what happens when we use the `n` command:

```
(Pdb) n
> at_content_function_pdb.py (30)<module>()
-> print("at content is " + str(at))
```

Chapter 2: Environments for developing in Python

`pdb` treats the `at_content()` function call as a single line and executes the whole function in one go, meaning that we don't have access to the variables `a` and `t` whose scope is limited to the function:

```
(Pdb) p a
*** NameError: NameError("name 'a' is not defined",)
(Pdb) p t
*** NameError: NameError("name 't' is not defined",)
```

To fix this we could exit the debugger, edit the code to move the `pdb.set_trace()` function inside the `at_content()` function and re-run the entire program. A better approach, however, would be to instruct `pdb` to step into the `at_content()` function the next time it's run. To do this we will use the `n` command to advance to the next iteration of the loop where we are just about to call the `at_content()` function:

```
(Pdb) n
at content is 0.1
...
(Pdb) n
...
(Pdb) n
...
(Pdb) n
...
(Pdb) n
> at_content_function_pdb.py (29)<module>()
-> at = at_content(cleaned)
```

At this point, rather than using the `n` command we will use the `s` command (short for *step into*):

```
(Pdb) s
--Call--
> at_content_function_pdb.py (4)at_content()
-> def at_content(dna):
```

Three interesting things happen here: we get the message `--Call--` telling us that we are calling a function; we get the name of the function appended to the status line; and the current line becomes the first line of the `at_content()` function. We can now use `n` to advance to the point where the A and T counts have been calculated:

```
(Pdb) n
> at_content_function_pdb.py (5)at_content()
-> a = dna.find("A")
(Pdb) n
> at_content_function_pdb.py (6)at_content()
-> t = dna.find("T")
(Pdb) n
> at_content_function_pdb.py (7)at_content()
-> at_content = (a + t) / len(dna)
```

and take a look at the `dna`, `a` and `t` variables:

```
(Pdb) p dna
'CGGCTGGTGTTAACGGCTAT'
(Pdb) p a
11
(Pdb) p t
4
```

Studying this output for a few moments will reveal that the counts are obviously wrong, and that what we have actually calculated is the position of the first T and A: we have accidentally used `find()` rather than `count()`. Fixing the code is just a matter of changing the function calls:

```
def at_content(dna):
    a = dna.count("A")
    t = dna.count("T")
    at_content = (a + t) / len(dna)
    return at_content
```

at_content_function_fixed.py

Doing more with pdb

In the previous collection of examples we've seen the features of pdb that will be useful in the vast majority of cases. However, there is more that pdb can do. The documentation[1] is brief by Python standards, but is worth reading if you find yourself using pdb a lot for debugging.

Among the advanced features are other ways of running pdb, the ability to examine variables at different points in the call stack, and the ability to set breakpoints that will only trigger under certain conditions. Since pdb is itself written in Python, it's also possible to extend it with custom code.

Alternatives to pdb

In the examples in this section we've concentrated on pdb because it's the most basic Python debugger, and because it's part of the Python Standard Library. However, there are many other Python debugging tools; which one you end up using largely depends on your programming environment.

Integrated development environments

If you're using an IDE (as discussed previously in this chapter) then it probably has a debugger built in, and it's probably a good idea to use it. Debuggers in IDEs tend to have a friendlier interface than the rather sparse interface that pdb offers, and most have additional features.

For example, PyCharm has a fully featured debugger built in with a graphical interface. The other third party IDE that we mentioned – Spyder – has a similar debugger interface that's actually built on pdb.

IDLE also has a graphical debugger built in which, though not as pretty as PyCharm's, is entirely functional – just go to the *Debug* menu to try it out.

---

1   https://docs.python.org/2/library/pdb.html

Command line debugging tools

Several tools exist that aim to give a more usable debugging interface on the command line. *Ipdb*[1] integrates features from the iPython command line shell[2] to add things like tab completion and syntax highlighting to the `pdb` interface. *Pdb++*[3] is another project that builds on `pdb` and adds similar features. Both ipdb and pdb++ preserve the command line interaction of `pdb` – you still have to type individual commands to control the debugger.

Pudb[4] takes things in a different direction by providing a graphical command line interface. Rather than issuing commands at a prompt, you interact with the debugger using keyboard shortcuts. Pudb also makes it easy to get an overview of a running program, and is a nice lightweight alternative to a full graphical debugger.

Standalone graphical debugging tools

If you don't want to do your debugging on the command line and would rather use a mouse-driven interface, take a look at *winpdb*[5], a cross platform graphical debugger. Winpdb requires a bit more installation than the command line tools mentioned above, but is a mature project.

Also worth a look is *bugjar*[6], a minimal graphical debugger that's currently lacking in documentation but is perfectly usable and can be installed with pip.

---

1 https://pypi.python.org/pypi/ipdb
2 Not to be confused with the iPython notebook, which we discussed in the chapter on development environments.
3 https://pypi.python.org/pypi/pdbpp
4 https://pypi.python.org/pypi/pudb
5 http://winpdb.org/
6 http://pybee.org/bugjar/

Chapter 2:Environments for developing in Python

Recap

The environment that we use for programming is one of the most personal and subjective decisions that we make. The set of tools that works well for one person may be a nightmare for others, and it's rare to come across two programmers who use exactly the same set up. While many programmers are perfectly productive with just a text editor, hopefully this chapter has given a overview of the tools that can make your life easier when writing code.

As is the case for most of this book, the utility of the tools that we've discussed will largely depend on the type of work you find yourself doing. The larger, more complex, and more collaborative your projects are, the greater the chances that the extra overhead of an integrated development environment will be worth it. And if you have to use lots of different Python programs or packages in your work, you'll find that working in virtual environments saves you many headaches.

As with many of the tools in this book, at first using a debugger seems like an inconvenience compared to simply using `print()` statements to track down bugs – and for small, simple programs it probably is. However, as programs get larger and more complicated the value of being able to step through a program, stop at particular points, examine variables and change the state of the program while it's running become extremely valuable.

The goal of the debugging section has not only been to introduce you to the specifics of how to run and interact with `pdb`, but to give an overview of the basic concepts of debugging and the terminology used. Whichever debugging tool you end up using in your work, they will all have the ability to set breakpoints, step into functions, and run a program line by line.

There's one final category of development tools which you need to know about, and that's **version control systems**. Version control systems are designed to solve the problem of multiple people working on a single software project, and are an absolutely essential tool for medium and large projects. We've avoided talking about version control in the main body of this chapter because there are many different version control systems, and they are language-agnostic – they work for all programming languages, and are not associated with Python specifically.

If you don't already have a favourite version control system, take a look at *git*[1], which is probably the current most popular system, and has ample documentation[2] and even an in-browser game to teach you how to use it[3].

---

1   https://git-scm.com/
2   https://git-scm.com/doc
3   https://try.github.io/levels/1/challenges/1

3: Organizing and sharing code

Introduction

As we work on a programming problem, our code generally goes through several stages. Most projects start out with some exploratory programming in an interactive environment like the Python shell or a notebook environment like iPython (as discussed in the previous chapter). Once we've figured out some code that works, we then make it permanent by turning it into a Python program which we can run on the command line. As the program grows in size and complexity, we may find that we need to add some structure – say, by turning some of it into functions, or by writing new classes[1].

For small, one off problems the process of code evolution generally stops there, but for more general purpose code there are two additional steps that we might want to take. Firstly, we might want to take a collection of useful functions and/or classes and turn it into a **module**, which allows us to reuse the code across multiple programs. Secondly, we might want to **package** and **distribute** the code so that other people can install and use it.

For those of us that use Python in a scientific setting, the idea of code reuse is particularly important. The nature of research work is such that we often spend our time writing programs to solve very similar problems[2], so having a quick and convenient way to reuse code can give us a big increase in productivity. In the same way, often several people in a research group

---

1 The best way to structure a program depends, of course, on the nature of the problem we're trying to solve.
2 If you're a bioinformatician, for instance, think about how many times you've written a program that does something to the headers of a FASTA file.

or institution are doing similar work and thus can benefit from a low friction way to share and reuse code.

The concept of publishing and distributing code is likewise of special interest to programmers working in a scientific context. For experimental research groups, projects generally result in the publication of results and data. For those of us working in bioinformatics, the equivalent is often the publication of methods, including computational methods and software tools . The ultimate goal, of course, is for other people to actually use your software and for this, it's important to make the process of downloading and installing it as straightforward as possible.

Thankfully, Python has excellent tools for packaging and distributing code. We'll start this chapter by looking at how we find, install and use modules in Python, then learn how to write our own modules.

Next, we'll look at Python's tools for package management and see how to distribute our code via the Python Package Index (PyPI) and install it using *pip*. This requires a bit more work by the package creator[1], but makes it very easy for others to install and use your code.

Programs, modules and packages

Before we start discussing modules and packaging, it's worth spending a bit of time thinking about the difference between a *program,* a *module* and a *package*. Most of the code we write in Python takes the form of *programs* i.e. text files containing Python code that run and do something useful.

A *module* is a piece of code which can be reused across multiple programs by importing it. Modules normally contain a bunch of functions or classes that are related to solving a particular type of problem. For instance, you've probably already encountered the `re` module, which contains functions

---

1   i.e. you.

Chapter 3:Organizing and sharing code

(like `re.search()` and `re.findall()`) that use regular expressions. Some modules – like `re` – are distributed along with Python, while others have to be installed separately.

The idea of a *package* in Python is a little more complicated. The simple explanation is that a package is just a way of collecting related modules together (for example, the *BioPython* package contains modules for reading sequence data, for running alignment algorithms, for working with protein structures, etc.). However, packages are also the basis of Python's distribution system (which we'll learn about in detail later in the chapter). If we want to take advantage of Python's tools to share code, then we need to turn our code into a package, even if that package contains just a single module.

In other programming languages, collections of reusable code are referred to as *libraries*, and you'll sometimes see this word used when discussing Python code. However, we'll try to avoid it in this chapter since it's less precise than *module* and *package*.

Working with modules

For the purposes of this discussion, we're going to think about two different types of modules.

Built in modules are those that are part of the standard Python distribution (often called the *Python standard library*). As you'd expect, built in modules are very mature and well documented and it's a good idea to use them wherever possible. Built in modules that you've probably already used include `re` for regular expressions, `sys` for interacting with the operating system, and `random` for generating random numbers. One of the nice things about using built in modules is that you can be confident that if you give a copy of a Python program to someone else, the built in modules will be available on the other person's computer without them having to do anything special[1].

Third party modules are those that are not part of the standard distribution and have to be installed separately. The maturity of third party modules varies greatly – some are long-standing projects with many contributors, others are just the result of an afternoon's programming. Modules that you create yourself will be classified as third party modules.

Built in modules

You've probably already used built in modules, so there's not too much that we need to say about them here. You use the `import` statement to make a module available in your program, then use the module name when you call a function from it:

```
import random

# simulate a die roll
print(random.choice(range(1,7)))
```

We might be curious about where the code for the `random` module actually resides. In order to find out, we can examine the module's `__file__` property in an interactive Python shell:

```
$ python
Python 2.7.6 (default, Jun 22 2015, 17:58:13)
...
>>> import random
>>> random.__file__
'/usr/lib/python2.7/random.pyc'
```

This tells us the file from which the module was loaded. In most cases this will be a *.pyc* file (which contains compiled Python code) rather than a *.py* file, but we can find the Python file by looking for the same filename

---

1   Assuming, of course, that they have installed Python!

Chapter 3:Organizing and sharing code

without the *c*. On my computer, I can view the code for the `random` module by opening the file:

```
/usr/lib/python2.7/random.py
```

The path will probably be different on your computer.

An obvious question at this point is to wonder how Python knows where to look for modules. The answer is that Python maintains an internal list of folders to search when you ask to import a module. A copy of this list is stored in the a variable called `path` in the `sys` module, so we can view it quite easily:

```
import sys
print sys.path
```

```
['/home/martin', '/usr/local/lib/python2.7/dist-packages/pip-6.1.1-
py2.7.egg', '/usr/lib/python2.7', ... ]
```

Just as before, this will look different on your computer[1]. Notice that the very first path in the list is the directory from which I ran the Python program (`/home/martin`) – this means that the first place Python looks for a module is in the current working directory.

You can find a list of the built in Python modules, along with documentation and examples, in the official Python docs:

```
https://docs.python.org/2/library/index.html
https://docs.python.org/3.4/library/index.html
```

One thing to be aware of is that code is added to the standard library on a regular basis, so older versions of Python might be lacking particular modules, functions or classes. For example, the `collections` module was

---

[1] In particular, it will look very different if you are using a virtual environment; see the section on virtual environments in the previous chapter for details.

added in Python 2.4, and the `collections.Counter` class was added in Python 2.7, so if you write a program that uses `collections.Counter`, it won't work under old versions of Python.

Third party modules

As we mentioned earlier, there are many different types of third party modules ranging from huge, international projects to tiny, one person projects. What all third party modules have in common is that they need to be installed before you can use them.

The problem of how best to install code libraries is one that every programming community has to deal with, and Python has been through several different solutions in its history. Given what we saw earlier about the Python search path, it's tempting to think that we can just download the module code and save it to one of the folders in the `sys.path` variable where Python will be able to find it. This approach will work for simple cases, but quickly becomes unmanageable in the real world. What happens when we want to install an updated version of a third party module? We have to be careful to remove the old one, and it's very easy to end up in a situation where we have multiple different versions of the same module installed. There is also the issue of dependencies, where one module relies on a second module and so we have to install them in the correct order.

The tool that the Python community has largely settled on to manage third party module installation is called *pip*. The pip tool is part of the standard Python installation from version 2.7.9, so if you have a recent version of Python installed then you probably already have *pip* (if not, you may have to install it[1]).

---

1   https://pip.pypa.io/en/stable/installing.html

Chapter 3:Organizing and sharing code

Pip makes it very easy to install third party modules (technically, when we use pip we are installing *packages* rather than *modules*). Let's look at an example – imagine we need to carry out some calculations involving dates and times. Python actually has a built in module called `datetime`[1] which works for simple calculations, but for more complicated tasks we need a more powerful module.

A good place to start looking for such a module is the list of useful modules on the Python wiki:

`https://wiki.python.org/moin/UsefulModules`

Browsing that page for a while will eventually lead us to a module called `dateutil`. The `dateutil` module is hosted on the Python Package Index[2] (often abbreviated to PyPI), a central repository of package information.

The `dateutil` page on PyPI[3] gives us a link to the documentation[4], and after reading it for five minutes we are convinced that it can help us and we want to install it. Going back to the PyPI page tells us that the actual name of the package is `python-dateutil`, so to install it all we need to do is run[5]:

```
$ pip install python-dateutil
```

pip will take care of downloading the code, putting in the right place, and making sure that any dependencies are installed. If we're curious, we can take a look at where the code ended up:

---

1 https://docs.python.org/2/library/datetime.html
2 https://pypi.python.org/pypi
3 https://pypi.python.org/pypi/python-dateutil
4 https://dateutil.readthedocs.org/en/latest/
5 On Linux and Mac computers, we may have to run pip as root, so the command line will be `sudo pip install python-dateutil`.

```
$ python
Python 2.7.6 (default, Jun 22 2015, 17:58:13)
...
>>> import dateutil
>>> dateutil.__file__
'/home/martin/lib/python2.7/site-packages/dateutil/__init__.pyc'
```

but in real world use, we generally don't care about the exact location, as long as the module is available for importing. We can also use pip to upgrade the package when a new version becomes available[1]:

```
$ pip install --upgrade python-dateutil
```

or to remove it if we decide it's not what we need:

```
$ pip uninstall python-dateutil
```

Not all packages can be installed in this way – some packages, particularly larger ones, rely on non-Python dependencies and so have a more complicated installation procedure. In general though, it's a good idea to use pip when we can. At the end of this chapter, we'll see how we can make it possible for other programmers to install **our** modules in this way.

Making a module

Now that we've seen how to make use of existing modules – both built in and third party – let's look at modules from the opposite angle: how to create a new module from scratch.

We'll start with a simple program that reads a DNA sequence from a file and prints its AT content[2]:

---

[1] Recall from the section on virtualenv in the chapter on development environments that we can also install modules into specific virtual environments.
[2] If you've read *Python for Biologists* or *Advanced Python for Biologists* then this example will be very familiar.

Chapter 3:Organizing and sharing code

```
from __future__ import division

# open the input file, read the contents and remove the newline
dna = open('dna.txt').read().rstrip("\n")

# calculate the AT content
length = len(dna)
a_count = dna.count('A')
t_count = dna.count('T')
at_content = (a_count + t_count) / length

# print the output
print("AT content is " + str(at_content))
```

There's a fairly obvious candidate for a function here: the bit of code that calculates the AT content, so we'll refactor it into a function where the argument is the DNA sequence and the return value is the AT content:

```
from __future__ import division

# calculate the AT content
def calculate_at(dna):
    length = len(dna)
    a_count = dna.count('A')
    t_count = dna.count('T')
    at_content = (a_count + t_count) / length
    return at_content

# open the input file, read the contents and remove the newline
dna = open('dna.txt').read().rstrip("\n")

# print the output
print("AT content is " + str(calculate_at(dna)))
```

At this point, we realize that the `calculate_at()` function is potentially useful in other programs. To reuse this function, we could simply copy and paste it, but hopefully you won't need too much convincing that this is a bad idea. Having multiple copies of the same code is inefficient and means that any changes to the code have to be made in multiple places.

Chapter 3:Organizing and sharing code

Instead, we'll move that function out of the program and into a module. Creating a module is just like creating a program – we make a new text file called *at_calculator.py* and paste the relevant code into it:

```
from __future__ import division

# calculate the AT content
def calculate_at(dna):
    length = len(dna)
    a_count = dna.count('A')
    t_count = dna.count('T')
    at_content = (a_count + t_count) / length
    return at_content
```
at_calculator.py

In the program file, we now have to `import` our new module, and use the module name when we call the function:

```
import at_calculator

# open the input file, read the contents and remove the newline
dna = open('dna.txt').read().rstrip("\n")

# print the output
print("AT content is " + str(at_calculator.calculate_at(dna)))
```
print_at.py

Notice that the module name **doesn't** include the *.py* part of the file name.

We can now happily write a new program that also uses the `calculate_at()` function just by importing the module:

Chapter 3:Organizing and sharing code

```
import at_calculator

# ask the user for a DNA sequence and filename
dna = raw_input("Enter a DNA sequence:\n")
output_filename = raw_input("Enter a filename:\n")

# write the AT content to the output file
with open(output_filename, "w") as out:
    out.write(str(at_calculator.calculate_at(dna)))
```

write_at.py

One final thing to note about our module: it begins with an `import` statement to import from the `__future__` module (to handle division in Python 2). This illustrates a general rule: any imports required by functions in a module need to be present in the module file, **not** in the program file. If we want floating point division in our program file, we have to include the line

```
from __future__ import division
```

in that file separately.

Names and namespaces

Notice how in the above examples, when we want to call the `calculate_at()` function we need to include the name of the module:

```
at_calculator.calculate_at("ACTGAC")
```

This seems annoying, but it's actually very useful because it means that we can have two functions with the same name[1], as long as they live in different modules. We say that each module has a different *namespace*, and

---

1   Or a function in a module with the same name as a built in function like `len()` or `print()`.

it's these different namespaces that allow different functions with the same name to coexist peacefully in the same program.

If we don't want to keep writing the name of the module every time we want to call the `calculate_at()` function, we can import the function like this:

```
from at_calculator import calculate_at
```

which allows us to call it without the module name like this:

```
calculate_at("ACTGATCGTCGAT")
```

This will work as long as there is no other function called `calculate_at()` in our program. If we **do** need to import two different functions with the same name but we **don't** want to use module names in the code, we can use the following workaround which assigns an alias to the function name:

```
from at_calculator import calculate_at as at1
from another_package import calculate_at as at2
...
at1("ACTGATGC")
```

but this is generally a bad idea: changing the name of a function makes code difficult to read.

Similarly, we can assign an alias to a module when we import it:

```
import at_calculator as atc
...
print(atc.calculate_at('ACTGATCGATCG'))
```

Chapter 3:Organizing and sharing code

which can sometimes help readability. Widely used modules sometimes have conventions about aliases – for example, the numpy module is always imported under the alias np:

```
import numpy as np
```

but in general aliases should be used with caution if you're expecting other people to read your code.

Documenting modules

Because modules typically hold a collection of related functions and classes[1], it often makes sense to add some general documentation to a module explaining its purpose. Python's *docstring* system works fine for annotating modules – we simply include a single string literal as the first line of the module. Because docstrings are often long enough to stretch over multiple lines, we generally write them with triple quotes:

```
"""
Functions for calculating metrics of DNA sequences

A collection of functions for calculating properties of DNA sequences.
Note: all functions assume upper case DNA sequence inputs.
"""

from __future__ import division

# calculate the AT content
def calculate_at(dna):
    ...
```

dna_metrics.py

---

1 Our AT content example only holds a single function, but your modules in the real world will be bigger.

Chapter 3: Organizing and sharing code

Of course, if we're using docstrings to annotate our module then we should probably switch to using them to annotate our functions as well:

```
def calculate_at(dna):
    """Return the AT content of the argument.
    Only works for uppercase DNA sequences
    """
    ...
```

dna_metrics.py

The big benefit of documenting our modules in this way is that it allows Python to display nicely formatted help messages:

```
$ python
Python 2.7.6 (default, Jun 22 2015, 17:58:13)
...
>>> import dna_metrics
>>> help(dna_metrics)
Help on module doc:

NAME
    dna_metrics - Functions for calculating metrics of DNA sequences

FILE
    /home/martin/python/dna_metrics.py

DESCRIPTION
    A collection of functions for calculating properties of DNA sequences.
    Note: all functions assume upper case DNA sequence inputs.

FUNCTIONS
    calculate_at(dna)
        Return the AT content of the argument.
        Only works for uppercase DNA sequences
```

Notice how in this interactive session Python's `help()` function automatically parses the first line of the module docstring as a short description and subsequent lines as an extended description. It also gathers the docstrings from individual functions to present a summary at the end of the help message.

Modules as programs

In the example above, there's a clear distinction between the module and the program that uses it. Occasionally, though, it's useful to be able to write a file that can be both run as a program, or imported as a module. This technique can be useful for a few different situations. For example, it allows us to write a module that runs a demonstration program to show off its features. Or we can write a module that, when run, executes some tests to make sure it's working properly. Other times, we have a useful program that we want to distribute, but we also want to allow other programmers to use its functions like a module.

The mechanism for having a module behave like a program[1] looks odd at first. It relies on the ability of a Python program to access its own name using the `__name__` variable:

```
print("my name is " + __name__)
```

This trick allows a module to determine whether it's being imported (in which case the `__name__` variable will be the name of the file, minus the *.py*) or run as a script (in which case the `__name__` variable will have the value `"__main__"`). To make use of this information, we can add an `if` statement that checks the value of `__name__` when the module is loaded and decides what to do:

```
if __name__ == "__main__":
    print("I am being run as a program!")
else:
    print("I am being imported as a module!")
```

In real life examples our modules don't need to do anything special if they're being imported, so we leave off the `else` clause. Here's an example

---

[1] Or having a program behave like a module, depending on your point of view.

using our AT content function. This version of the code will ask the user for a DNA sequence then print out the AT content if it's run as a program, but if it's imported it will just make the `calculate_at()` function available as normal:

```
from __future__ import division

# calculate the AT content
def calculate_at(dna):
    length = len(dna)
    a_count = dna.count('A')
    t_count = dna.count('T')
    at_content = (a_count + t_count) / length
    return at_content

if __name__ == "__main__":
    dna = raw_input("Enter a DNA sequence:\n").rstrip("\n")
    print("AT content is " + str(calculate_at(dna)))
```

at_calculator_script.py

Executing code in modules

In our AT calculator example above, the code inside the `if` statement only executes when the module is run as a program. Sometimes, however, we need to run some code in order to initialize the module – code which must run before we can use any of the module's functions.

Let's look at an example: here's a module for carrying out DNA to protein translation. It has a single function, `translate_dna()`, which takes a DNA string as its argument and returns a protein string:

Chapter 3:Organizing and sharing code

```python
"""Functions for translating DNA sequences"""

def translate_dna(dna):
    """Return the translation of a DNA sequence"""

    # define a dict to hold the genetic code
    gencode = {
        'ATA':'I', 'ATC':'I', 'ATT':'I', 'ATG':'M',
        'ACA':'T', 'ACC':'T', 'ACG':'T', 'ACT':'T',
        'AAC':'N', 'AAT':'N', 'AAA':'K', 'AAG':'K',
        'AGC':'S', 'AGT':'S', 'AGA':'R', 'AGG':'R',
        'CTA':'L', 'CTC':'L', 'CTG':'L', 'CTT':'L',
        'CCA':'P', 'CCC':'P', 'CCG':'P', 'CCT':'P',
        'CAC':'H', 'CAT':'H', 'CAA':'Q', 'CAG':'Q',
        'CGA':'R', 'CGC':'R', 'CGG':'R', 'CGT':'R',
        'GTA':'V', 'GTC':'V', 'GTG':'V', 'GTT':'V',
        'GCA':'A', 'GCC':'A', 'GCG':'A', 'GCT':'A',
        'GAC':'D', 'GAT':'D', 'GAA':'E', 'GAG':'E',
        'GGA':'G', 'GGC':'G', 'GGG':'G', 'GGT':'G',
        'TCA':'S', 'TCC':'S', 'TCG':'S', 'TCT':'S',
        'TTC':'F', 'TTT':'F', 'TTA':'L', 'TTG':'L',
        'TAC':'Y', 'TAT':'Y', 'TAA':'_', 'TAG':'_',
        'TGC':'C', 'TGT':'C', 'TGA':'_', 'TGG':'W'}

    last_codon_start = len(dna) - 2
    protein = ""

    # for each codon in the dna, append an amino acid to the protein
    for start in range(0,last_codon_start,3):
        codon = dna[start:start+3]
        amino_acid = gencode.get(codon.upper(), 'X')
        protein = protein + amino_acid

    return protein
```

dna_translation.py

Just like our AT content example, we can write a small program that imports the module and uses the function:

```
import dna_translation

dna = raw_input("Enter a DNA sequence:\n").rstrip("\n")
print(dna_translation.translate_dna(dna))
```

This works fine for a small test program that just translates a single DNA sequence, but there's a fairly glaring inefficiency in the module – the dict that holds the genetic code is rebuilt every time the `translate_dna()` function is called. Given that the contents of this dict never need to change, it would be better to create it once when the module is imported, then it can be used for all future calls to `translate_dna()`.

Making the change is simple; we just move the dict definition from inside the function and place it at the top level of code. We'll also add a `print()` statement to print the length of the dict:

```
# define a dict to hold the genetic code
gencode = {
    'ATA':'I', 'ATC':'I', 'ATT':'I', 'ATG':'M',
    ...

print("gencode stores " + str(len(gencode)) + " codons")

def translate_dna(dna):
    ...
```

dna_translation_efficient.py

Now the `gencode` dict will be created as soon as the module is imported. We can demonstrate this by starting an interactive session and importing the module – notice that the size of the dict is printed **before** we ever call the `translate_dna()` function:

Chapter 3:Organizing and sharing code

```
$ python
Python 2.7.6 (default, Jun 22 2015, 17:58:13)
...
>>>import dna_translation_efficient
gencode stores 64 codons
>>>dna_translation_efficient.translate_dna("ATCGATCGATCGA")
'IDRS'
```

This kind of initialization code is very useful where there's some code which needs to be run before the functions in the module can be used. In the above example, there's no drawback to creating the dict as soon as the module is imported, since it needs to be created in order for the `translate_dna()` function to work.

Be wary of using this approach when the requirements of the module are not so straightforward. If our module contained a collection of functions, only some of which needed the `gencode` dict, then it wouldn't be a good idea to create it when the module is imported, since it might never be needed. Unnecessary initialization code can slow down the import process.

For a module where a large data structure is required for only some functions a more sophisticated approach is needed – either having a function which the program code can call to explicitly create the data structure, or checking for the existence of the data structure inside the functions that use it and creating it only if necessary.

Packages

If we take the idea of modules a step further, we end up with the concept of a *package*. Just as a module is a convenient way to gather together multiple related functions and classes, a package is a way to gather together multiple related modules.

From a strictly organizational point of view it's generally only necessary to add the extra structure of a package for large, complex libraries – most libraries can happily exist in a single module. However, creating a package is also the easiest way to make your library installable, so when you come to the point of distributing your module you will need to build a package, even if it only holds a single module.

To turn our DNA translation module into a package, we create a new folder whose name will be the package name, then move our module inside it. We also have to add a special file called *__init__.py* to the folder, which just acts as a placeholder to tell Python that the folder is a package.

If we create a folder called *dnatools*, move our file *dna_translation.py* inside it, and create an empty file called *__init__.py*, then we'll have a new package called `dnatools` which contains our module – the folder structure looks like this:

```
dnatools/
    __init__.py
    dna_translation.py
```

We can import and use the module exactly as before, with the addition of the package name:

```
import dnatools.dna_translation
print(dnatools.dna_translation.translate_dna("ACTGTGAC"))
```

More interestingly, we can now start to distribute our package for other people to use.

Distributing code

Now that we've covered modules and packages, we can tackle the problem of distributing our code. As you're probably aware, distributing a standalone Python program is easy – just send somebody a copy of the program file (or have them download it from a website). This straightforward approach works fine for Python programs that only use modules from the standard library.

If you've written a program that uses some third party modules then the distribution requirements become a bit more complicated; at the very least you'll need to include some instructions which tell the user which other modules they need to install.

If you decide to split some of your program code into a separate module to make it easier to manage, then distributing your program becomes a bit more complicated still – now the end user has to download a small collection of files rather than just one, so you'll probably need to bundle them together somehow[1]. But the process from the end user's point of view is still simple: download the files then run the program.

At this point, however, we run into the same problems that we discussed earlier when talking about installing third party modules – how does the user upgrade to a new version of your module when one becomes available, and how do they take care of dependencies? The solution is to take advantage of *pip* to make your module easily installable.

In the last section of this chapter, we'll see how to upload our package to PyPI, the Python Package Index, making it possible for anyone in the world to download and install it with a single command. Compared to most languages, the process of distributing our modules in Python is very simple, thanks largely to the tools that come as part of Python.

Preparing for distribution

Before we can upload our package, there are a few preliminary steps.

First, we'll need to create an account on the PyPI server, which we can do by going to the main page[2] and following the "Register" link.

---

1   For example, by creating a *.zip* file.
2   https://pypi.python.org/pypi

Chapter 3: Organizing and sharing code

Next, we'll need to add another layer to our folder structure. In order to keep everything organized, we want the bits of code that are necessary to use our libraries (i.e. all the stuff we've written so far) to be separate from the bits that are involved with distributing it (i.e. the stuff we're about to create). To do this, we'll take our existing folder *dnatools*, which contains *__init__.py* and *dna_translation.py*, and put it inside another folder, which we'll also call *dnatools*. The folder structure now looks like this:

```
dnatools/
    README.txt
    dnatools/
        __init__.py
        dna_translation.py
```

and the top-level *dnatools* folder is where we'll be working from now on. You'll find this complete folder structure inside the exercises folder for this chapter.

Notice that in the folder structure above we've also created a *README.txt* file. This isn't strictly necessary, but it's definitely best practice and failing to do so will cause warnings later on. For this example, we'll just put a single line of text in our *README.txt* file:

```
A package for DNA sequence manipulation
```

For real life packages, your *README.txt* can contain as much documentation as you think is useful.

Finally, we need to create a program called *setup.py*. This program has two jobs: it stores metadata about our package (more on that below), and it allows us to execute the commands necessary to register and upload our package. The structure of the *setup.py* file is always the same:

Chapter 3:Organizing and sharing code

```
from setuptools import setup

setup(name='dnatools',
      version = '0.1',
      description = 'Functions for working with DNA sequences',
      url = 'http://example.com',
      author = 'Martin Jones',
      author_email = 'martin@pythonforbiologists.com',
      license = 'MIT',
      packages = ['dnatools'])
```

dnatools/setup.py

It just imports the `setup()` function from the `setuptools` module, then calls that function. The interesting part is the arguments to the `setup()` function, which contain all the important information about our package.

The `name`, `version` and `description` arguments are pretty self explanatory – they contain the name of the package, the version number and a one line description. Next comes the `url` argument, which is normally a link to the homepage of your package or the source code repository. The next two arguments – `author` and `author_email` – contain your own contact information. The `license` argument contains the name of the license that your code is under.

The final argument, `packages`, is a list of the folders which contain Python modules that we want to include in the distribution. For our example we have just a single folder, called `dnatools`, but for more complex projects there might be several.

Strictly speaking, the only argument to the `setup()` function that's absolutely necessary is `name` (and later on `version`, when we want to update a package). However, it's considered best practice to include all of the arguments in the example above.

One very important argument that we've not used in the example above is the `install_requires` argument, which is a list of dependencies for our package. Our DNA translation module doesn't require any other packages to work, but if it did, we could list them using this argument to ensure that they are installed along with our package. For example, if our package relied on the `requests` module, we would add the following argument to our `setup()` function call:

```
from setuptools import setup

setup(name = 'dnatools',
      version = '0.1',
      description = 'Functions for working with DNA sequences',
      url = 'http://example.com',
      author = 'Martin Jones',
      author_email = 'martin@pythonforbiologists.com',
      license = 'MIT',
      packages = ['dnatools'],
      install_requires = ['requests'])
```

This is a very useful feature to have, because it allows the Python package manager to automatically install dependencies whenever a user installs our package. Remember that we don't need to include modules from the standard library in this list.

Registering, building and uploading

With these preparations out of the way, we can begin the task of releasing our package to the wider world. Initially, this is a two step process: we must first register our package (which reserves the name), then create a source distribution (which bundles our code up into a single archive file) and upload that source distribution (which puts it on PyPI and makes it available for others to install).

There's quite a lot of complexity involved at both these steps but, happily, most of it is hidden from us – our *setup.py* program does the hard work for us. To register the package, we run *setup.py* with the *register* command. Here's how it looks on a Linux or Mac system:

```
$ python setup.py register
```

It will look a little different on Windows. This command uses the metadata that we entered earlier to create a package on PyPI. During this process, we'll be asked for the username and password for our PyPI account. If, when we run this command, we get a message stating that we are not allowed to store information, it's likely that we've accidentally chosen a package name that already exists, so we'll have to pick a new one.

Once the *register* command has executed, we can build a source distribution and upload it. To do this, we run *setup.py* again, this time with the *sdist upload* command:

```
$ python setup.py sdist upload
```

This command bundles all our folders and files into a single archive file and uploads this archive file to PyPI.

It's important to note that we only have to register the package the **first** time we want to upload it. For subsequent updates, we only have to run the *sdist upload* command (though we do need to remember to increase the version number each time we update the package).

Once we've successfully uploaded our package, it should be possible to install it on any properly set up computer by simply running

```
$ pip install dnatools
```

Try it now on your computer[1].

---

1   Depending on your system this may require special permissions: if you're on a Linux or Mac system, try `sudo pip install dnatools`.

Complicating factors

The process outlined above is sufficient for simple cases, and will cover the vast majority of what we want to do with packages and modules. However, there are a number of potential complications that are well outside the scope of this book. If you need to do any of the following:

- distribute a package with dependencies that are not on PyPI
- include a test suite as part of your package
- include command line tools along with your package
- include data files along with your package
- include code written in a non-Python language as part of your package
- tell `setup()` to include/exclude specific files when it builds the distribution
- create a Windows installer or a Linux rpm/deb for your package

then you'll need to dive into the `distutils` documentation[1].

Recap

In this chapter, we've looked at two separate but closely related concepts: how to reuse code by turning it into modules and packages, and how to distribute those packages using the Python Package Index. If you're feeling confused about which technique you need, see which of the following scenarios matches your needs....

1. If you want to distribute **a program that only uses built in modules**, then all you need to do is make your Python program file available for download, and all the end user needs to do is run it.

---

1 https://docs.python.org/2/distutils/index.html

Chapter 3:Organizing and sharing code

2. If you want to distribute **a program that uses third party modules** (e.g. `dateutil`), then you need to make your Python program file available for download and also include documentation telling the user which extra extra modules they need to install.

3. If you want to distribute **a module that you have written**, then you need to turn it into a package and upload it to PyPI.

4. If you have **written a program and moved some of the code into a module**, then you have two choices. If you're reasonably sure that the module is only useful for this specific program, then simply create a *.zip* file that contains both and make it available for download (along with instructions to install any non-built-in modules that your program also uses). If, on the other hand, you think the module might be useful for other programs, then distribute the module (as in scenario 3) and the program (as in scenario 2) separately.

5. If you have **written a module and you want to use it in multiple programs of your own, but you don't want to distribute it**, then you can just install it on your own computer by following the instructions for distributing a package above, but running:

```
$ python setup.py install
```

instead of carrying out the registration/upload steps. You will probably find, however, that eventually you want to run your programs on a different computer, at which point it's probably a good idea to upload the module to PyPI.

4: Testing your code

Introduction

The idea of testing your code to see what it does is a pretty obvious thing to do when you start learning programming, and consequently the phrase "testing code" can have many meanings. At the simple end of the scale, testing is anything that you do to verify that your code is working correctly – if you've ever typed something like this:

```
for line in open("somefile.txt"):
    # check that the file is opening correctly
    print(line)

    # real code to process the line goes here...
```

then you've engaged in testing. At the most sophisticated end of the scale, testing can involve purpose built libraries, dedicated testing servers, and developers whose full time job is building and running tests. There's a steady progression between these two extremes of simple and sophisticated tests.

For the vast majority of scientific programming projects the sweet spot for testing lies somewhere in the middle and it's on that area that we'll be concentrating in this chapter: ways of testing code that are more structured and automated than those in the example above, but not so heavy duty that they require a dedicated team of programmers!

The chapter is divided into two broad sections. First, we'll look at a bunch of basic concepts behind testing, using the simplest testing tool available to us – Python's built in `assert` statement. We'll examine different types

Chapter 4: Testing your code

of tests, see the kinds of problems that testing can help us to avoid, and look at some best practices when writing tests.

In the second part of the chapter, we'll introduce a more sophisticated testing tool called nose, which will make it easier to follow the principles outlined in the first section. There are many testing frameworks for Python, of which nose is just one – it strikes a nice balance between power and ease of use, and is likely to be suitable for most programming projects you'll encounter. At the end of the chapter, we'll mention a few scenarios in which nose might not be the right tool for the job and look at which different testing frameworks we might choose.

You may notice that many of the examples we used in this chapter resemble those from the section on debugging in the first chapter. This is not a coincidence; the ideas of debugging and testing are closely linked. When we identify a failing test we often use a debugger to track down the source of the problem, and when we spot a bug using the debugger we typically add a test to alert us if it reoccurs in the future.

Testing with assert

Let's start with a simple challenge: write a function which takes a DNA sequence, a kmer length and a threshold, and returns a list of all the kmers that occur more than the threshold number of times in the sequence[1]. Here's a first attempt:

---

[1] By a kmer we simply mean a short section of DNA which is **k** bases long – so if **k** is 3 we are looking at 3mers, if **k** is 5 we are looking at 5mers, etc.

Chapter 4: Testing your code

```
def find_common_kmers(dna, k, threshold):
    result = []   ❶
    for start in range(len(dna)):   ❷
        kmer = dna[start:start+k]   ❸
        if dna.count(kmer) >= threshold:   ❹
            result.append(kmer)
    return result
```

find_common_kmers.py

We create a `result` list to hold the kmers❶, then iterate over each of the possible kmer start positions using a `range()`❷. For each start position, we calculate the stop position by adding `k` to the start. We then use the start and stop positions to extract the kmer from the DNA sequence❸. We append the kmer to the result list **only** if the number of times the kmer appears in the DNA sequence is greater than or equal to the threshold❹.

This looks pretty good, so we can go ahead and see if it works. We'll set the kmer size to 3 and the threshold to 2, and make up a short DNA sequence that contains the 3mer "atg" twice. Can our function correctly figure out which kmer occurs twice?

```
print(find_common_kmers('atgaatgc', 3, 2))
```

```
['atg', 'atg']
```

Straight away, the output throws up an interesting question: is this the result we wanted? Our function has certainly returned the correct 3mer, but it is present twice in the output (because it occurs twice in the input DNA sequence). This result is interesting because there's no obvious way to say whether this behaviour is correct or not; it depends on what we want to use the output for.

Chapter 4: Testing your code

What we have actually discovered here is an ambiguity in the way the original problem was described – if you read back over the challenge description you'll see that it never stated whether the output should only contain unique kmers or not. This brings us to the first benefit of testing: it forces us to think very precisely about how we want our code to behave.

To keep things interesting, let's say for the purposes of this example that we decide we don't want any duplicate kmers in the output. At this point, we could go back and edit the function so that it works like this – but a better idea might be to write an `assert` statement which tests for the behaviour we want:

```
assert find_common_kmers('atgaatgc', 3, 2) == ['atg']
```

An `assert` statement (sometimes referred to simply as an *assertion*) is a condition that should always be true – in this case, that our function run with a particular input should always produce a particular output. When we run this line of code, the `assert` keyword at the start of the line will cause Python to evaluate the condition and throw an error if it's false. With the function in its current state, the assertion fails and Python tells us that the function has not produced the right output by displaying an `AssertionError`:

```
AssertionError
    Traceback (most recent call last)
----> 1 assert find_common_kmers('atggatgcgctcggt', 3, 2) == ['atg']
```

If we now go back and edit the function so that it only adds a kmer to the result if its count is above the threshold **and** it does not already appear in the result:

Chapter 4: Testing your code

```
def find_common_kmers(dna, k, threshold):
    result = []
    for start in range(len(dna)):
        kmer = dna[start:start+k]
        if dna.count(kmer) >= threshold and kmer not in result:
            result.append(kmer)
    return result
```

find_common_kmers_no_duplicates.py

then we can run the assertion again and this time it produces no errors.

An obvious question at this point is: why should we bother writing an assertion if we're going to fix the code anyway? We'll see the reasoning behind this later in the chapter.

Now let's try our function out on a slightly longer sequence. Here's an example of a function call using a made up DNA sequence where the "atg" 3mer occurs 3 times, with `k` and `threshold` both set to 3:

```
find_common_kmers('atgaatgcaaatga', 3, 3)
```

What will the output from this function call be? A valuable mental exercise is to think about the expected output **before** we run the code. By writing the expected output in the form of an assertion, we can make a statement about the expected behaviour of the function and then see if the actual output matches up, rather than just running the code and seeing what happens. Think of it as being like the difference between running an experiment to test a particular hypothesis, as opposed to running it just to gather data.

Here's what we expect our function to return, written as an assertion:

```
assert find_common_kmers('atgaatgcaaatga', 3, 3) == ['atg']
```

Chapter 4:Testing your code

The expected output is exactly the same as in the previous example – there is only one 3mer that occurs at least 3 times. This assertion fails, and if we look at the returned value from the function we can see why:

```
['atg', 'a']
```

We have discovered a bug in the way that our function generates the kmers. On the last iteration of the `for` loop, the value of `start` will be 13 (one less than the length of the DNA sequence), so `kmer` will be equal to `dna[13:16]`, which gives us the single character string `'a'`. Because `'a'` occurs 7 times in the DNA sequence, it gets added to the `result` list.

The fix for this bug is simple; we just have to make sure that every start position is at least `k` bases away from the end of the DNA string. One way to do this is to check this condition for each iteration of the `for` loop:

```
def find_common_kmers(dna, k, threshold):
    result = []
    for start in range(len(dna)):

        # are we at least k bases away from the end of the DNA string?
        if len(dna) - start > k - 1:
            ...
```

but a more elegant way to do it is to adjust the argument to `range()` so that it doesn't generate those last few start positions:

```
def find_common_kmers(dna, k, threshold):
    result = []
    for start in range(len(dna) + 1 - k):
        ...
```

find_common_kmers_correct_range.py

Now both of our assertions run without errors.

The two fixes that we've made so far illustrate how we can use assertions to identify bugs and unexpected behaviour in our functions, so it seems like a good idea to write some more. If we start doing so:

```
assert find_common_kmers('atgaatgcaaatga', 3, 3) == ['atg']
assert find_common_kmers('atgaatgc', 3, 2) == ['atg']
assert find_common_kmers('ctagctgctcgtgactgtcagtgtacg', 2, 4) ==
    ['ct', 'tg', 'gt']
assert find_common_kmers('cccaaaacccaaaacccaaaacccaaaa', 4, 4) ==
    ['ccca', 'ccaa', 'caaa', 'aaaa']
...
```

we can see that it quickly becomes overwhelming: there are obviously an infinite number of possible inputs for us to test. Rather than trying to test them all, the trick to efficient testing is to test the behaviour of the function on the extremes of inputs. If we know that our function works when the kmer size is 1, and we know that it works when the kmer size is 10, we can be reasonably confident that it will work for any number in between:

```
assert find_common_kmers('aattggcc', 1, 2) == ['a', 't', 'g', 'c']
assert find_common_kmers('tagctagtcg', 10, 1) == ['tagctagtcg']
```

A good place to find examples of strange behaviour and bugs in our functions is by trying unrealistic inputs. For example, what do we expect as the output if we supply a kmer length of zero? Even though this question doesn't make any biological sense, our function has to return something. The most sensible answer is probably an empty list[1]:

```
assert find_common_kmers('tagctagtcg', 0, 2) == []
```

but currently this assertion fails. The actual output is a list with a single element which is an empty string:

---

1   Later in the chapter we'll see that raising an exception is also a valid response.

Chapter 4: Testing your code

```
['']
```

To understand why we get this output, we need to think about what happens when we try to get a kmer of length zero. Consider the first iteration of the `for` loop: `start` will be 0 so the first kmer will be `dna[0:0]`, which evaluates to an empty string. What then happens when we use `count()` to figure out the number of times the empty string appears in the DNA sequence? The answer is always one greater than the length of the DNA sequence (think of it as finding one occurrence of the empty string in between each pair of adjacent characters, plus one each at the start and the end). In the above example, the DNA sequence is 10 bases long, so the count for the empty string is 11 which is greater than the threshold so the empty string is added to the `result` list.

This is an example where testing has revealed an unexpected behaviour which might have surprised even experienced Python programmers. The easiest way to fix the behaviour is to put in a special case at the start of the function which returns an empty list if the kmer length is less than one (this will also take care of negative kmer lengths):

```python
def find_common_kmers(dna, k, threshold):
    if k < 1:
        return []
    result = []
    for start in range(len(dna) + 1 - k):
        kmer = dna[start:start+k]
        if dna.count(kmer) >= threshold and kmer not in result:
            result.append(kmer)
    return result
```

find_common_kmers_fix_empty.py

We now have a collection of assertions that test a range of different inputs:

```
assert find_common_kmers('atgaatgcaaatga', 3, 3) == ['atg']
assert find_common_kmers('atgaatgc', 3, 2) == ['atg']
assert find_common_kmers('aattggcc', 1, 2) == ['a', 't', 'g', 'c']
assert find_common_kmers('tagctagtcg', 10, 1) == ['tagctagtcg']
assert find_common_kmers('ctagctgctcgtgactgtcagtgtacg', 2, 4) ==
    ['ct', 'tg', 'gt']
assert find_common_kmers('cccaaaacccaaaacccaaaacccaaaa', 4, 4) ==
    ['ccca', 'ccaa', 'caaa', 'aaaa']
assert find_common_kmers('tagctagtcg', 0, 2) == []
assert find_common_kmers('tagctagtcg', -3, 2) == []
```

find_common_kmers_fix_empty.py

all of which are successfully handled by the final version of our function. A collection of assertions like this is often called a *test suite*. A test suite like this one is designed to test the behaviour of a piece of code under many different scenarios.

Refactoring and regression testing

Take another look at the `find_common_kmers()` function above. How long do you think it will take to run on different inputs – in other words, if we double the length of the DNA sequence, what will happen to the execution time? The `for` loop will run twice as many times[1], so we might expect the function to take twice as long to execute. However, if we look inside the `for` loop, we can see a process that is also affected by the length of the sequence. Doubling the length of the DNA sequence will cause `dna.count(kmer)` to take twice as long, because there are twice as many positions to check.

This pattern – a method call that takes twice as long, being executed twice as many times – might cause us to expect that doubling the length of the DNA sequence will **more** than double the execution time, and we'd be

---

[1] In fact, slightly less than twice because of the fixed padding at the end, but this will be negligible provided the sequence is much longer than `k`, so it doesn't affect our reasoning.

Chapter 4:Testing your code

right. On my computer, finding all 8mers that occur at least a thousand times in a 20 kilobase sequence takes just over half a second, but if we double the sequence length to 40 kilobases the execution time jumps to two and a half seconds.

This slowdown is obviously going to cause a problem when we want to process very large input sequences, so we'd like to rewrite the function. For this example, rewriting the function is quite straightforward – we have never actually written a full program that uses it so, if we like, we can redesign the function from scratch. However, imagine the real world scenario in which we have already written a program that uses the function several times. In this situation, we have to be much more careful when rewriting the function. If we change its behaviour – for example, by making it return a dict rather than a list, or by swapping round the order of the arguments – we will break our existing code.

What we need to do is to change the way that the function works **internally** without changing any of its **external** behaviour. In other words, we want to keep the function arguments and return values exactly the same, and just change the code inside the function. This is a very powerful technique in programming and has a special name: *refactoring*.

Here's an attempt at refactoring our `find_common_kmers()` function - notice that the function arguments and return value are exactly the same as the old version:

```
def find_common_kmers(dna, k, threshold):

    kmer2count = {}  ❶
    for start in range(len(dna) + 1 - k):❷
        kmer = dna[start:start+k]
        old_count = kmer2count.get(kmer, 0)❸
        kmer2count[kmer] = old_count + 1

    result = []
    for kmer, count in kmer2count.items():❹
        if count >= threshold:
            result.append(kmer)
    return result
```

find_common_kmers_fast.py

This version of the function takes a different approach to solving the problem. First, we build up a dict❶ where the keys are the kmers and the values are counts. The logic for iterating over each individual kmer is exactly the same as before❷. For each kmer, we look up the current count with a default of zero❸ then add one and update the dict to store the new count. When we've finished iterating over the kmers, we now have a total count for each kmer stored in the dict[1]. This approach avoids the need to repeatedly run `dna.count()` inside the `for` loop.

Once we've finished building the dict, we iterate over it once❹, check each value to see if it's greater than or equal to the threshold, and if it is, add the kmer to the `result` list.

A quick timing test shows that this new function has fixed our slowdown problem: the 20 kilobase sequence now takes 9 milliseconds to run and the 40 kilobase sequence takes 18 milliseconds. Not only is the function much faster in absolute terms, but the time now scales linearly with the length of the sequence.

---

[1] There is a built in Python data structure which is designed to do this – `collections.Counter` – but rather than use it I have written the logic out here in full to make it easier to follow.

Chapter 4:Testing your code

We've successfully followed the first rule of refactoring – changing the way that the function works internally – but how do we know whether we've been successful in the second part: keeping the external behaviour the same? It's at this point that our test suite becomes incredibly useful; we can simply run it using our new function and if we get any errors, we know that we have changed something about the behaviour.

When we run our assertions with the new function, we notice something interesting right away: the first two assertions – where there is a single element in the return value – pass, but the third one fails:

```
AssertionError
        Traceback (most recent call last)
----> 3 assert find_common_kmers('aattggcc', 1, 2) == ['a', 't', 'g', 'c']
```

Looking at the actual output from the function call reveals why:

```
['a', 'c', 't', 'g']
```

Although the output contains the correct kmers (in this case, single bases) the order is different. In the first version of the function, the kmers would always be returned in the order they first appear in the sequence, but in this new version the order is effectively random[1]. Once again, the nature of testing forces us to think a bit more deeply about the behaviour we want: do we actually care about the order of the kmers in the result? In this case the answer is probably no – we are interested in the set of common kmers and the order in which they appear is irrelevant.

To reflect the fact that we don't care about the order, we can alter the assertions by transforming all the lists to sets using the `set()` function[2]:

---

[1] The order is actually determined by the order in which keys are stored in the dict, but since this order is undefined we can't rely on it.
[2] Another way to do this would be to change the output of `find_common_kmers()` to be a set

Chapter 4: Testing your code

```
...
assert set(find_common_kmers('aattggcc', 1, 2)) == set(['a','t','g','c'])
...
```

Unlike lists, sets are inherently unordered so now our assertions will test that the output contains the correct elements without regard for the order, and the above assertion now passes without error.

Running the modified test suite reveals another interesting failure – the new function fails to give the correct answer when we supply a kmer length of zero:

```
AssertionError
        Traceback (most recent call last)
----> 6 assert set(find_common_kmers('tagctagtcg', 0, 2)) == set([])
```

Once our attention has been drawn to this bug, we can spot the cause in the code quite easily. It's the same problem as we had in the original function, which caused us to write this specific test in the first place: with a kmer length of zero, we get a single empty string as the output. Just as before, the fix is to check for this special case at the start of the function:

```python
def find_common_kmers(dna, k, threshold):
    if k < 1:
        return []

    kmer2count = {}
    ...
    return result
```

find_common_kmers_fast_fix_empty.py

This scenario – where refactoring the code reintroduces a bug that was previously fixed – is so common that it has a special name; we call it a *regression*. Finding the regression in this way – by running our test suite –

---

rather than a list, but this would count as changing its behaviour.

dramatically demonstrates the value of testing. We have uncovered a bug in our new function **without** writing any additional code, and **before** running it on real data (and possibly introducing errors in our results). This idea of catching bugs before they have any consequences is a powerful one and lies at the heart of automated testing.

This also explains why, when we first encountered the bug in the old version of the function, we chose to write a test which exposes it rather than simply fixing the function. If we had just fixed the function and not bothered to write a test, then we wouldn't have been able to identify the bug so quickly in the new version of the function.

The fixed version of the new function successfully passes all the tests (and so does the original version, even though we've changed the tests to use sets rather than lists). Thanks to our test suite, we can now confidently use our new version of the function as a replacement for the old version, which means that all existing code which currently uses the old version will benefit from the improved performance.

Set up and tear down

The kmer counting function that we've been looking at so far has a particular property that makes it easy to test: it doesn't have any side effects. In other words, the only way that information gets into the function is via the arguments, and the only way that information gets out of the function is via the return value. It doesn't make use of any non-argument variables, and it doesn't affect any variables that may be defined outside it[1].

---

[1] In programming, functions that have these properties are called *pure*. See the chapter on functional programming in *Advanced Python for Biologists* for a detailed description of these properties.

Chapter 4:Testing your code

Let's now look at what happens when we try to test a function that **does** have side effects. Imagine we want to write a function that will take a list of short DNA sequence reads and remove any that contain more than a certain number of undetermined bases (represented by 'N'). It's tempting to write something like this:

```
def filter_reads(reads, threshold):
    for read in reads:
        if read.count('N') >= threshold:
            reads.remove(read)
```

but this is a bad idea as we're removing elements from the `reads` list at the same time we are iterating over it. Instead, we need to iterate over a copy of the list like this[1]:

```
def filter_reads(reads, threshold):
    for read in list(reads):
        if read.count('N') >= threshold:
            reads.remove(read)
```

filter_reads.py

Let's write a few tests using `assert`. We'll create a list of three made up reads with zero, one and two undetermined bases, then check that using various thresholds removes the correct reads. Firstly, running the function with a threshold of one should remove both of the reads that contain N:

```
reads = ['ATCGTAC', 'ACTGNTTACGT', 'ACTGNNTACTG']

# remove reads with a threshold of one
filter_reads(reads, 1)
assert reads == ['ATCGTAC']
```

---

1   In the real world we would probably use a list comprehension here, but the code presented here is fine as an example.

Chapter 4:Testing your code

Notice that because our `filter_reads()` function doesn't return a value we can't write the `assert` statement in one line as we did in the previous example – instead, we have to create the list, call the function, then check the value of the list.

This first assertion passes without error, so we can go on and write some more – running the function with a threshold of two should cause only the last read to be removed:

```
reads = ['ATCGTAC', 'ACTGNTTACGT', 'ACTGNNTACTG']
filter_reads(reads, 2)
assert reads == ['ATCGTAC', 'ACTGNTTACGT']
```

and running it with a threshold of three should leave the list unchanged:

```
reads = ['ATCGTAC', 'ACTGNTTACGT', 'ACTGNNTACTG']
filter_reads(reads, 3)
assert reads == ['ATCGTAC', 'ACTGNTTACGT', 'ACTGNNTACTG']
```

These three assertions all pass without error, but when we look at the testing code, there's something unsatisfying:

```
reads = ['ATCGTAC', 'ACTGNTTACGT', 'ACTGNNTACTG']
filter_reads(reads, 1)
assert reads == ['ATCGTAC']

reads = ['ATCGTAC', 'ACTGNTTACGT', 'ACTGNNTACTG']
filter_reads(reads, 2)
assert reads == ['ATCGTAC', 'ACTGNTTACGT']

reads = ['ATCGTAC', 'ACTGNTTACGT', 'ACTGNNTACTG']
filter_reads(reads, 3)
assert reads == ['ATCGTAC', 'ACTGNTTACGT', 'ACTGNNTACTG']
```

filter_reads.py

The line that creates the `reads` list is repeated three times, once for each test. As we add more tests, we're going to have to add more copies of this line, which makes the test code hard to read. For this example it's not too bad, since we only need a single line of code to create the `reads` list, but imagine a more complicated example that required five lines of set up code for each test. We can't simply create the list once and reuse it across all tests like this:

```
reads = ['ATCGTAC', 'ACTGNTTACGT', 'ACTGNNTACTG']

filter_reads(reads, 1)
assert reads == ['ATCGTAC']

# reads is now ['ATCGTAC']
filter_reads(reads, 2)
assert reads == ['ATCGTAC', 'ACTGNTTACGT']

filter_reads(reads, 3)
assert reads == ['ATCGTAC', 'ACTGNTTACGT', 'ACTGNNTACTG']
```

because by the time we get to the second function call, we have already removed the last two reads from the list. What we need is a way of resetting the list back to a known starting state before each test. One option is to define a function whose job is to set up the starting conditions for each test:

Chapter 4:Testing your code

```
reads = []
def create_reads():
    global reads
    reads = ['ATCGTAC', 'ACTGNTTACGT', 'ACTGNNTACTG']

create_reads()
filter_reads(reads, 1)
assert reads == ['ATCGTAC']

create_reads()
filter_reads(reads, 2)
assert reads == ['ATCGTAC', 'ACTGNTTACGT']

create_reads()
filter_reads(reads, 3)
assert reads == ['ATCGTAC', 'ACTGNTTACGT', 'ACTGNNTACTG']
```

filter_reads_setup.py

Notice how we have to use the `global` keyword to make sure that the `reads` variable name inside the function refers to the `reads` variable created at the start of the program rather than creating a new `reads` variable.

At first glance, this is not much better than the previous code – it's even longer, and we still have to explicitly call the `create_reads()` function before each test. However, it's arguably easier to read – the purpose of the function call is clearer than in the previous version, and any further complexity that we need to add to the set up code will be contained within the `create_reads()` function. A piece of data created in order to run tests like this is often called a *fixture*.

Automated testing with `nose`

At this point in the chapter, we've seen how to create individual tests, how tests work to track down bugs and prevent regressions, and how testing a range of different inputs exposes the behaviour of code under circumstances that we might not have thought of. Now it's time to put these ideas to use in a framework that's designed to make testing easier.

`nose`[1] is a testing framework that allows us to easily define, run and summarize tests as long as they follow certain conventions. Setting up our tests to use `nose` involves a bit more work than just using `assert` but, as we'll see, there are some big benefits to doing so.

To see how `nose` works, let's go back and recreate the tests from the first example we looked at in this chapter – the `find_common_kmers()` function. There are two important conventions we need to be aware of: files that contain test code should start with the word `test`, and each test should be in a function whose name also starts with the word `test`. We'll create a new file called *test_kmer_function.py*, add the very first version of our function definition at the start, and create a new function which carries out the first test in our test suite:

```
def find_common_kmers(dna, k, threshold):
    result = []
    for start in range(len(dna)):
        kmer = dna[start:start+k]
        if dna.count(kmer) >= threshold:
            result.append(kmer)
    return result


def test_3mers():
    assert(find_common_kmers('atgaatgcaaatga', 3, 3) == ['atg'])
```

test_kmer_function.py

Notice that although we have put this test inside a function definition – and consequently have had to come up with a name for it – the `assert` statement is exactly the same as before. Also note that although for this example we have included the function definition at the start of the test

---

1 https://nose.readthedocs.org/en/latest/

file, in real life projects we will probably store the function definition in a module and `import` it[1].

We already know that this test is going to fail because of the bugs that we found earlier in the chapter, but let's run it anyway to see what happens. Rather than running

```
$ python test_kmer_function.py
```

which won't do anything because the code doesn't actually call the `test_3mers()` function, we'll use the `nosetests` tool. To run the tool we just run the command

```
$ nosetests test_kmer_function.py
```

and `nosetests` will run each of the functions in the file that start with the word `test`. If we simply run `nosetests` without a filename argument, it will find all files that start with the word "test" and process them all, but that's not very useful here as our examples folder contains several different test files.

As expected, our test fails:

```
$ nosetests test_kmer_function.py
F
======================================================================
FAIL: test_kmer_function.test_3mers
----------------------------------------------------------------------
Traceback (most recent call last):
...
    assert(find_common_kmers('atgaatgcaaatga', 3, 3) == ['atg'])
AssertionError

----------------------------------------------------------------------
Ran 1 test in 0.004s

FAILED (failures=1)
```

---

[1] Take a look at the chapter on organizing and sharing code for details of how to do this.

but the output is a bit more interesting than our earlier examples. It tells us the name of the test that failed (`test_3mer`) and the name of the file (`test_kmer_function`). It also tells us how many tests passed and failed (in this case just one) and how long it took to run the tests (0.004 seconds).

To make the output even more useful, we can switch from using `assert` to using the special testing functions that are provided by `nose`. The `assert_equal()` function takes two arguments and tests whether or not they are equal. It's part of the `nose.tools` package, so we have to import it at the start of the test file. After rewriting the `test_3mer()` function to use `assert_equal()` the code looks only slightly different:

```
from nose.tools import assert_equal

def find_common_kmers(dna, k, threshold):
    ...

def test_3mers():
    assert_equal(find_common_kmers('atgaatgcaaatga', 3, 3), ['atg'])
```

test_kmer_function_equal.py

but when we run `nosetests`, the output is dramatically improved:

Chapter 4:Testing your code

```
$ nosetests test_kmer_function_equal.py
F
======================================================================
FAIL: test_kmer_function_equal.test_3mers
----------------------------------------------------------------------
...
    assert_equal(find_common_kmers('atgaatgcaaatga', 3, 3), ['atg'])
AssertionError: Lists differ: ['atg', 'atg', 'atg', 'a'] != ['atg']

First list contains 3 additional elements.
First extra element 1:
atg

- ['atg', 'atg', 'atg', 'a']
+ ['atg']

----------------------------------------------------------------------
Ran 1 test in 0.005s

FAILED (failures=1)
```

In addition to the extra information from the previous example, the output from nosetests now tells us

- what caused the error i.e. the fact that the lists differed
- what the expected and actual outputs were
- how many additional elements were in the actual output
- the value of the first extra element in the actual output

All of these extra bits of information can be useful when we're trying to track down the cause of the error. In particular, being able to see the actual output removes the need to go back and run the function call separately like we had to earlier.

In this case the error is caused by the two problems we discussed earlier in the chapter: we didn't ensure that output elements are unique, and we didn't exclude incomplete kmers from the end of the sequence. Updating the function to fix these two bugs – just like we did before – fixes the error:

Chapter 4:Testing your code

```
from nose.tools import assert_equal

def find_common_kmers(dna, k, threshold):
    result = []
    for start in range(len(dna) + 1 - k):
        kmer = dna[start:start+k]
        if dna.count(kmer) >= threshold and kmer not in result:
            result.append(kmer)
    return result

def test_3mers():
    assert_equal(find_common_kmers('atgaatgcaaatga', 3, 3), ['atg'])
```

test_kmer_function_unique.py

Another nice feature of `nose` is that, unlike `assert`, it doesn't immediately stop after the first failed test. To see why this is useful, let's add the rest of our test suite to the *test_kmer_function_unique.py* file and rewrite the assertions to use `assert_equal()`:

Chapter 4:Testing your code

```python
from nose.tools import assert_equal

def find_common_kmers(dna, k, threshold):
    result = []
    for start in range(len(dna) + 1 - k):
        kmer = dna[start:start+k]
        if dna.count(kmer) >= threshold and kmer not in result:
            result.append(kmer)
    return result

def test_3mers():
    assert_equal(find_common_kmers('atgaatgcaaatga', 3, 3), ['atg'])

def test_low_threshold():
    assert_equal(find_common_kmers('atgaatgc', 3, 2) , ['atg'])

def test_single_bases():
    assert_equal(find_common_kmers('aattggcc', 1, 2) ,
                 ['a', 't', 'g', 'c'])

def test_whole_sequence():
    assert_equal(find_common_kmers('tagctagtcg', 10, 1) , ['tagctagtcg'])

def test_long_sequence():
    assert_equal(find_common_kmers('ctagctgctcgtgactgtcagtgtacg', 2, 4),
                 ['ct', 'tg', 'gt'])

def test_long_sequence_4mers():
    assert_equal(find_common_kmers('cccaaaacccaaaacccaaaacccaaaa',4, 4) ,
                 ['ccca', 'ccaa', 'caaa', 'aaaa'])

def test_zero_length_kmer():
    assert_equal(find_common_kmers('tagctagtcg', 0, 2) , [])

def test_negative_length_kmer():
    assert_equal(find_common_kmers('tagctagtcg', -3, 2) , [])
```

Running nosetests again, we see the output summarized for all tests. To avoid running the tests in previous versions of the file, we'll pass a filename to nosetests:

```
$ nosetests test_kmer_function_unique.py
......FF
======================================================================
FAIL: test_kmers.test_zero_length_kmer
----------------------------------------------------------------------
Traceback (most recent call last):
  ...
    assert_equal(find_common_kmers('tagctagtcg', 0, 2) , [])
AssertionError: Lists differ: [''] != []

First list contains 1 additional elements.
First extra element 0:


- ['']
+ []


======================================================================
FAIL: test_kmers.test_negative_length_kmer
----------------------------------------------------------------------
Traceback (most recent call last):
  ...
    assert_equal(find_common_kmers('tagctagtcg', -3, 2) , [])
AssertionError: Lists differ: [''] != []

First list contains 1 additional elements.
First extra element 0:


- ['']
+ []


----------------------------------------------------------------------
Ran 8 tests in 0.007s

FAILED (failures=2)
```

We see that two out of our eight tests failed and, just as before, for each failed test we see the difference between the expected and actual output. This helps us to quickly spot that the tests involving zero or negative kmer lengths are returning empty strings and, just as before, we can fix the bug by adding a special case at the start of the function.

Chapter 4:Testing your code

For our final look at this example, let's see what happens when we replace the `find_common_kmers()` function with our more efficient refactored version:

```
from nose.tools import assert_equal

def find_common_kmers(dna, k, threshold):
    if k < 1:
        return []

    kmer2count = {}
    for start in range(len(dna) + 1 - k):
        kmer = dna[start:start+k]
        old_count = kmer2count.get(kmer, 0)
        kmer2count[kmer] = old_count + 1

    result = []
    for kmer, count in kmer2count.items():
        if count >= threshold:
            result.append(kmer)
    return result

def test_3mers():
    assert_equal(find_common_kmers('atgaatgcaaatga', 3, 3), ['atg'])

...
```

test_kmer_function_fast.py

Recall from earlier in the chapter that this new version causes the kmers to appear in the results in a different order than they appear in the DNA sequence. The output from `nosetests` makes this easy to spot – here are just the relevant lines:

```
AssertionError: Lists differ: ['a','c','t','g'] != ['a','t','g','c']
AssertionError: Lists differ: ['gt','tg','ct'] != ['ct','tg','gt']
AssertionError: Lists differ: ['caaa','aaaa' ...] != ['ccca','ccaa',...]
```

which make it obvious that the correct kmers are being returned but in a different order. Just as before, it's probably more useful to interpret this as

113

Chapter 4: Testing your code

an error in the tests rather than in the code, and just as before, we can fix the tests by turning the lists into sets before comparing them:

```
...

def test_single_bases():
    assert_equal(set(find_common_kmers('aattggcc', 1, 2)) ,
            set(['a', 't', 'g', 'c']))

...
```

Set up and tear down

Now we've seen what `nose` can do, let's see how it copes with our second example from this chapter, the `filter_reads()` function. Creating a new file called *test_filter_reads.py*, adding the function definition, and rewriting our tests to use `assert_equals()` gives us this:

Chapter 4:Testing your code

```
from nose.tools import assert_equal

def filter_reads(reads, threshold):
    for read in list(reads):
        if read.count('N') >= threshold:
            reads.remove(read)

reads = []
def create_reads():
    global reads
    reads = ['ATCGTAC', 'ACTGNTTACGT', 'ACTGNNTACTG']

def test_threshold_one():
    create_reads()
    filter_reads(reads, 1)
    assert_equal(reads,  ['ATCGTAC'])

def test_threshold_two():
    create_reads()
    filter_reads(reads, 2)
    assert_equal(reads,  ['ATCGTAC', 'ACTGNTTACGT'])

def test_threshold_three():
    create_reads()
    filter_reads(reads, 3)
    assert_equal(reads,['ATCGTAC', 'ACTGNTTACGT', 'ACTGNNTACTG'])
```

test_filter_reads.py

which works as expected (remember to run it with

```
nosetests test_filter_reads.py
```

so we don't accidentally run the other test files). Because the idea of a function that sets up test conditions is a common one in testing, `nose` supports a special type of annotation for defining which set up function a given test depends on. To use it, we import `with_setup` from the `nose.tools` package, then add a special line before each test function definition line:

```
from nose.tools import assert_equal
from nose.tools import with_setup

def filter_reads(reads, threshold):
    for read in list(reads):
        if read.count('N') >= threshold:
            reads.remove(read)

reads = []
def create_reads():
    global reads
    reads = ['ATCGTAC', 'ACTGNTTACGT', 'ACTGNNTACTG']


@with_setup(create_reads)
def test_threshold_one():
    filter_reads(reads, 1)
    assert_equal(reads,  ['ATCGTAC'])

@with_setup(create_reads)
def test_threshold_two():
    ...

@with_setup(create_reads)
def test_threshold_three():
    ...
```

test_filter_reads_setup.py

A line that begins with @ is called a *decorator*, and is used to supply some extra information about a function – in this case, it tells `nose` that it needs to run `create_reads()` before carrying out each test.

We also have the option of specifying a function to be run after each test has been completed[1]. This can be useful for tests that create resources (temporary files and directories, database connections, large data structures in memory, etc.) which have to be freed. For example, imagine a function that takes a single integer argument and creates a bunch of new

---

1   Known as a *tear-down* function.

Chapter 4: Testing your code

folders with integers as names. We might write a test that calls the function before checking for the existence of the new directories:

```
import os
from nose.tools import assert_equals

def make_dirs(n):
    for i in range(n):
        os.mkdir(str(i))

def test_make_three_folders():
    make_dirs(3)
    for i in range(3):
        assert_equals(os.path.exists(str(i)), True)
```

The function and test both work fine, but after the test has finished the newly created directories are still there, which may cause problems later on. In particular, any tests that run after this one and attempt to create a folder with the same name as an existing one will raise an error.

A clean up method, along with a `@with_setup` decorator, takes care of the problem in an elegant way which keeps the clean up code separated from the testing code:

Chapter 4: Testing your code

```
import os
from nose.tools import assert_equals
from nose.tools import with_setup

def remove_folders():
    "delete all folders whose name is a single character"
    for name in os.listdir("."):
        if len(name) == 1:
            os.rmdir(name)

def make_dirs(n):
    ...


@with_setup(teardown=remove_folders)
def test_make_three_folders():
    ...
```

test_make_folders.py

Notice how we use the `teardown` keyword argument to the `@with_setup` decorator. This tells `nose` that after the `test_make_three_folders()` function has been run, the `remove_folders()` function must be run before any other tests can take place.

One final note on set up and tear-down functions: they tend to be most useful when testing the behaviour of classes. Classes are inherently *stateful*[1] – when we create an instance of a class and then call methods on it, the methods generally act by manipulating the state (i.e. the instance variables) of the object. This means that when testing the behaviour of a class we have written, we generally need a set up method which creates an instance of that class with a known starting state.

On the other hand, set up and tear-down functions are **never** needed when testing code that is stateless, i.e. code that consists of pure functions. If we

---

1   For an introduction to Python's class system, see the chapter on object oriented programming in *Advanced Python for Biologists*.

Chapter 4:Testing your code

take our `filter_reads()` function from before and rewrite it so that it returns a filtered copy of the input list rather than altering the list itself:

```
def filter_reads(reads, threshold):
    result = []
    for read in list(reads):
        if read.count('N') < threshold:
            result.append(read)
    return result
```

Then we have turned `filter_reads()` into a pure function and can test it without worrying about setting up the input data each time:

```
from nose.tools import import assert_equal

def filter_reads(reads, threshold):
    ...

reads = ['ATCGTAC', 'ACTGNTTACGT', 'ACTGNNTACTG']

def test_threshold_one():
    assert_equal(filter_reads(reads, 1), ['ATCGTAC'])

def test_threshold_two():
    assert_equal(filter_reads(reads, 2), ['ATCGTAC', 'ACTGNTTACGT'])

def test_threshold_three():
    assert_equal(filter_reads(reads, 3),
            ['ATCGTAC', 'ACTGNTTACGT', 'ACTGNNTACTG'])
```

The ease of testing pure functions is often cited as an argument in favour of a functional style of programming.

Types of assertions

So far in our discussion of nose, we've been using `assert_equals()` to describe the expected behaviour of our tests. This works fine, but

occasionally we can take advantage of more specific functions offered by
`nose.tools`. For example, our test which checks for the existence of
folders in the above example would be better written using
`assert_true()`:

```
import os
from nose.tools import assert_true

def make_dirs(n):
    for i in range(n):
        os.mkdir(str(i))

def test_make_three_folders():
    make_dirs(3)
    for i in range(3):
        assert_true(os.path.exists(str(i)))
```

This version of the test has the exact same meaning but has two important advantages: it's clearer to read, and can give more helpful output. As you might expect, there are a whole family of `assert_something()` functions which we can use in this way[1]. The most widely used tend to be

- `assert_equal()`
- `assert_true()`
- `assert_in()` to test if an element is in a list
- `assert_is_instance()` to test whether a value is of a specific type.

There are also negated versions of these (`assert_not_equal()`, `assert_not_in()`, etc.) along with a few specialized ones like

---

[1] This is probably the best place to find a list:
https://docs.python.org/2/library/unittest.html#assert-methods
but note that we spell them differently when using nose e.g. `assert_equals()` rather than `assertEquals()`

Chapter 4:Testing your code

`assert_regexp_matches()` and `assert_dict_contains_subset()`.

To see the value in having all these functions, lets look at the different ways we could test that the output of a function is always greater than five. We could simply write:

```
assert_equals(some_function(foo, bar) > 5, True)
```

or even

```
assert_true(some_function(foo, bar) > 5)
```

but the clearest version – and the one that will give the most useful output during testing – uses the `assert_greater()` function:

```
assert_greater(some_function(foo, bar), 5)
```

On a similar theme, consider these three different ways of specifying that a particular function should always return a valid base:

```
assert_equals(some_function(foo, bar) in ['A', 'T', 'G', 'C'], True)
assert_true(some_function(foo, bar) in ['A', 'T', 'G', 'C'])
assert_in(some_function(foo, bar), ['A', 'T', 'G', 'C'])
```

These three lines all express the exact same test, but look at the different error messages we get when the output from `some_function()` is "B":

```
AssertionError: False != True
AssertionError: False is not true
AssertionError: 'B' not found in ['A', 'T', 'G', 'C']
```

It's easy to see how the third, most specific test produces the most useful output.

There's even a function that tests if the set of items in two lists are the same without regard for order – `assert_items_equal()` – which allows us to write our tests from the kmer counting example much more concisely:

```
...
def test_single_bases():
    assert_items_equal(find_common_kmers('aattggcc', 1, 2),
                       ['a', 't', 'g', 'c']))
...
```

In addition to being more concise, this is easer to read – when we see that we are using `assert_items_equal()` we immediately understand that we are comparing items without regard for order.

Tests and numbers

You may have noticed that none of the examples of testing we've looked at so far have involved numbers. The reason we've waited so long to discuss testing numerical output is that it forces us to confront some surprising behaviour in the way that Python handles numbers. Limitations in the accuracy of floating point numbers (i.e. those with a decimal place) mean that small errors often creep in when we carry out calculations in Python. For the simplest demonstration of this, try to calculate the sum of 0.1 and 0.2 using Python:

```
>>> 0.1 + 0.2
0.30000000000000004
```

Chapter 4:Testing your code

A full explanation for this error is beyond the scope of this book[1]. The simple explanation is that some numbers can't be represented exactly in binary (which is how computers store data). Errors accumulate when a mathematical calculation in our program involves one of these numbers.

For testing purposes, all we need to know is that whenever we carry out floating point calculations with Python, we must bear in mind that the answers we get may have small errors. Most of the time this isn't a problem – as we can see from the example above, the deviation of the actual result from the expected one is very small. It becomes a problem, however, when we start to do comparisons between numbers:

```
>>> 0.1 + 0.2 == 0.3
False
```

Since testing involves comparing expected to actual results, floating point errors can cause tests to fail even when the code is correct. For example, here's a function that calculates the AT content of a DNA sequence by adding together the fraction of bases that are A and the fraction of bases that are T:

```
from __future__ import division
def calculate_at(dna):
    a_fraction = dna.count('a') / len(dna)
    t_fraction = dna.count('t') / len(dna)
    return a_fraction + t_fraction
```

The function works correctly, but floating point errors mean that the output may not exactly match our expectations. With a ten base DNA sequence that contains one A and two Ts the output is not exactly the same as the correct answer:

---

1   The Python documentation has a very readable explanation:
     https://docs.python.org/2/tutorial/floatingpoint.html

```
>>> calculate_at("ccacttgcgg")
0.30000000000000004
```

and if we try to write a test that involves this input sequence:

```
from nose.tools import assert_equal
assert_equal(calculate_at("ccacttgcgg"), 0.3)
```

it will fail:

```
AssertionError: 0.30000000000000004 != 0.3
```

This is a particularly awkward problem to address, since the function will pass a very similar test if, by chance, we happen to pick an input that doesn't introduce any numerical errors:

```
assert_equal(calculate_at("ctcgtagtca"), 0.5)
```

To address this problem, `nose.tools` provides a special `assert_almost_equals()` function. As the name suggests, it checks that the two arguments are equal to within some small amount of variation (by default, seven decimal places):

```
from nose.tools import assert_almost_equal
assert_almost_equal(calculate_at("ccacttgcgg"), 0.3)
```

Using `assert_almost_equal()` rather than `assert_equal()` when testing numerical functions will avoid spurious errors caused by floating-point limitations[1].

---

[1] If you genuinely need a level of floating point accuracy beyond that which Python normally offers, take a look at the `decimal` module.

Chapter 4:Testing your code

Testing exceptions

We've seen in the examples above how to test several different types of behaviour that we might expect from functions. The last type of tests that we need to look at are those that involve a key aspect of a function's behaviour – raising exceptions. A detailed explanation of Python's exception handling system is beyond the scope of this book[1] – all we need to know is that when it comes to a function's behaviour, raising the correct exception when something goes wrong is just as important as returning the correct answer.

Take a look at this version of `find_common_kmers()` that takes a stricter approach to dealing with invalid kmer lengths:

```python
def find_common_kmers(dna, k, threshold):

    if not isinstance(k, int):
        raise TypeError("kmer length must be an integer")
    if k < 1:
        raise ValueError("kmer length must be a positive integer")

    result = []

    kmer2count = {}
    for start in range(len(dna) + 1 - k):
        kmer = dna[start:start+k]
        old_count = kmer2count.get(kmer, 0)
        kmer2count[kmer] = old_count + 1


    for kmer, count in kmer2count.items():
        if count >= threshold:
            result.append(kmer)

    return result
```

find_common_kmers_exceptions.py

---

1   For a detailed description see the chapter on exceptions in *Advanced Python for Biologists*.

This version of the function carries out two checks on the `k` argument before starting the calculation. First, it checks that `k` is an integer (and not a floating point number, a string, etc.) and if not, raises a `TypeError`. Second, it checks that `k` is greater than zero and if not, raises a `ValueError`.

Trying a few function calls with invalid kmer length arguments illustrates how the function works:

```
>>> find_common_kmers("atcgttacgatgatcgctaac", 1.5, 2)
TypeError: kmer length must be an integer
>>> find_common_kmers("atcgttacgatgatcgctaac", -2, 2)
ValueError: kmer length must be a positive integer
```

Notice that both input checks are necessary; a value for `k` of 1.5 will be caught by the first check but not the second (since it's greater than one) while a value for `k` of -2 will be caught by the second check but not the first (since it is an integer).

Just as with other aspects of the function's behaviour, we'd like to write tests which check that it raises the correct exceptions in response to different types of invalid input. Remember, though, that what we see in the output above isn't actually the return value of the function, so we can't do this:

```
def test_non_integer_input():
    assert_equal(find_common_kmers("atcgttacgatgatcgctaac", 1.5, 2),
                "TypeError: kmer length must be an integer")
```

Instead, we must use the special `assert_raises()` function. This is an unusual type of assertion function because it takes a variable number of arguments. The first argument is the type of exception that we expect to be raised, the second argument is the name of the function that we want to test, and the remaining arguments are the arguments with which we want to call the function we are testing:

Chapter 4:Testing your code

```
from nose.tools import assert_raises

def test_non_integer_input():
    assert_raises(TypeError, find_common_kmers, "atcgttactaac", 1.5, 2)

def test_invalid_integer():
    assert_raises(ValueError, find_common_kmers, "atcgttcgctaac", -2, 2)
```

`find_common_kmers_exceptions.py`

Designing for testing

Once we introduce testing as part of our code development process, ease of testing becomes an important factor when we are thinking about how to design a piece of code. Take a look at this function which calculates the average number of Ns per line in a text file containing DNA sequences:

```
from __future__ import division

def average_ns(filepath):
    input_file = open(filepath)
    total_n_count = 0
    total_line_count = 0

    for line in input_file:
        total_line_count = total_line_count + 1
        total_n_count = total_n_count + line.count('N')

    input_file.close()
    return total_n_count / total_line_count
```

The code itself is straightforward; we open the file and iterate over the lines, keeping a running total of both the number of lines and the number of Ns, then calculate the mean number of Ns per line and return the result. Now let's say we want to test this function – how could we do it?

One approach is to create a test file called *test.dna* with the contents:

```
ACTCGNAAGN
ATCCGT
TATACGN
```

and place it in the same folder as the code, then write the test as normal:

```
from nose.tools import assert_equal
def test_three_lines():
    assert_equal(average_ns("test.dna"), 1)
```

However, there are two problems with this. One is that the test code is no longer self contained – it relies on the *test.dna* file being available, and if this file is moved or altered then the tests will fail even though the code is still fine. The second problem is that the testing code will be slow. Reading and writing to files is generally slow compared to other operations. This isn't a problem for a single test like the one above, but imagine a test suite with many such tests. If running a test suite takes a long time, then it's tempting to skip it.

We could get around the first problem by getting creative with a set up method which writes the necessary file out before running the test:

```
from nose.tools import assert_equal
from nose.tools import with_setup

def create_test_input():
    test_input = open("test.dna", "w")
    test_input.write('ACTCGNAAGN\n')
    test_input.write('ATCCGT\n')
    test_input.write('TATACGN\n')
    test_input.close()

@with_setup(create_test_input)
def test_three_lines():
    assert_equal(average_ns("test.dna"), 1)
```

but this might still fail for a filesystem related reason (e.g. no space left on the disk, the user doesn't have permissions to create a file) and it makes

Chapter 4:Testing your code

the speed even worse because now we have to both read and write a file to carry out the test.

A better way to fix the problem is to slightly redesign the `average_ns()` function so that instead of taking a file path as its argument, it takes an iterable object:

```
def average_ns(data):
    total_n_count = 0
    total_line_count = 0
    for line in data:
        total_line_count = total_line_count + 1
        total_n_count = total_n_count + line.count('N')
    return total_n_count / total_line_count
```

To test this new version of the code, we can simply supply the lines as a list:

```
def test_three_lines():
    assert_equal(average_ns(['ACTCGNAAGN','ATCCGT','TATACGN']), 1)
```

but because of Python's iterator interface, we can also supply an open file object which will behave like a list of lines:

```
average_ns(open("somefile.dna"))
```

This approach allows us to test the function using input data as a list (thus neatly avoiding the problems with the file testing approach), while still being able to use it to process files in real word programs.

If we really want our function to take a file path as its argument, we can rename `average_ns()` to make clear that it's a helper function – and should not be called directly – by prefixing it with an underscore[1]:

```
def _average_ns(data):
    total_n_count = 0
    total_line_count = 0
    for line in data:
        total_line_count = total_line_count + 1
        total_n_count = total_n_count + line.count('N')
    return total_n_count / total_line_count
```

then writing a wrapper function which takes a file path as its argument, opens the file, and passes the open file to `_average_ns()` to do the actual computation:

```
def average_ns_in_file(filepath):
    f = open(filepath)
    return _average_ns(f)
```

This design allows us to test the `_average_ns()` function using a list as input, while still allowing us to write code which uses the `average_ns_in_file()` function.

---

1   This is a Python convention: names that begin with an underscore should be treated as an implementation detail i.e. should not be used directly by calling code.

Chapter 4: Testing your code

Special types of testing

The tools and techniques in this chapter will likely be suitable for the vast majority of scientific computing projects. However, certain situations require more specialized approaches. We'll finish this chapter by looking at scenarios in which you'll need to reach for slightly different testing tools.

Testing behaviour of object oriented code

For the sake of readability, all of the example code we've been testing in this chapter has been written as functions. However, exactly the same testing strategies apply to code that resides in classes. Generally, when testing object oriented code, we'll create an instance of our class then test each of its methods in a separate function. For example, imagine we have written a `DNASequence` class whose constructor takes a DNA string as its argument, and which has `get_at_content()` and `get_reverse_complement()` methods[1]. If we're using `nose` for testing, then a test file for such a class might look like this:

---

1 Take a look at the chapter on object oriented programming in *Advanced Python for Biologists* for a detailed description of this example.

```
from nose.tools import assert_equal
from nose.tools import with_setup
from mypackage import DNASequence

my_sequence = None
def create_sequence():
    global my_sequence
    my_sequence = DNASequence("ATGC")

@with_setup(create_sequence)
def test_get_at_content():
    assert_equal(my_sequence.get_at_content(), 0.5)

@with_setup(create_sequence)
def test_reverse_complement():
    assert_equal(my_sequence.get_reverse_complement(), "GCAT")
```

As we add more complex behaviour to the class definition, we'll add tests to the end of the file. Notice that although the code we're testing is written as a class, the tests themselves are just written as normal functions. It is possible to write nose tests using classes[1] and it might be useful to do so if you are testing a very complex class hierarchy.

Mocking complex objects for testing

One of the reasons that we've concentrated on simple functions for our examples of testing is that it has allowed us to write tests that are minimally reliant on the outside world and hence are easy to comprehend. In real world code, however, this won't always be the case. For example, imagine you have written a function that, given a DNA sequence accession number as its argument, connects to a sequence database server, downloads the relevant DNA sequence record, and returns the sequence as a string:

---

[1] You can find an overview here:
http://nose.readthedocs.org/en/latest/writing_tests.html#fixtures

Chapter 4:Testing your code

```
def retrieve_dna(accession):

    # make a connection to the server
    ...

    # download the record
    ...

    # extract the sequence from the record
    ...

    # return the DNA sequence
```

Writing a test for such a function seems quite straightforward; we pick an accession number for which we know the correct sequence, call the function with it as input, and check the response:

```
assert_equal(retrieve_dna("1234"), "ACTGCTAGCTCGATGC...")
```

However, we run into the same problem as with our test file example above: there are many potential factors outside the code which could cause this test to fail. For instance, the tests might be run on a computer that doesn't have access to the internet, or the server might be briefly down for maintenance. Just as with the file example, the best solution is to separate out the code that connects to the server and downloads the record into a separate function:

```
def retrieve_dna(accession):

    record = download_record_from_server(accession)

    # extract the sequence from the record
    ...

    return dna_sequence
```

then have two versions of the `download_record_from_server()` function – one "fake" version to use for testing (which doesn't actually connect to the server but just returns the record) and one "real" version to use in real programs. This technique is called *mocking*, and the standard Python module for doing so is called `mock`[1].

Testing user interfaces

The examples we've seen in this chapter are best characterized as *unit tests* – they aim to test a single small piece of functionality. For simple programs and libraries, unit testing will be all we need, but for larger programs we may need other types of tests. Tests that are more complicated than unit tests are generally divided into two categories – *integration tests* and *functional tests*.

While unit tests aim to test the behaviour of a small unit of code – typically a single function or method – *integration tests* (as the name suggests) aim to test the behaviour of a collection of functions or classes working together, and *functional tests* aim to test the behaviour of a complete program[2]. These categories are somewhat fuzzy, so the distinction between integration and functional tests is not sharply defined.

A particularly interesting type of functional test is one intended to check the behaviour of a graphical or web-based user interface. When building Python programs with graphical or web interfaces it's often straightforward to write unit tests for the functions and methods that actually do the computational work, but the tools we've looked at so far in this chapter are not able to test the interface.

To test a graphical or web interface, we need a tool that's capable of simulating the behaviour of a user interacting with the interface. There are a range of suitable specialized testing tools for this and the best one to use will depend on the specifics of the program you are testing. The main

---

1   https://pypi.python.org/pypi/mock
2   Note that the word "functional" here has nothing to do with functional programming.

Chapter 4:Testing your code

Python website hosts lists of tools for testing graphical[1] and web[2] interfaces. It's worth noting that many Python web frameworks also include functional testing tools.

Performance testing

Tools written for bioinformatics generally fall into two categories when it comes to performance. One the one hand, we have simple housekeeping scripts for which performance doesn't matter at all. On the other hand, we have complicated algorithms for which performance may be a very important consideration. For the latter type of code, we sometimes want a way of checking whether a change to the code has made it run more slowly (just as we use normal unit tests to check whether a change to the code has introduced any bugs). For this purpose we can use the special `@timed` decorator provided by `nose`. `@timed` takes an argument which is the number of seconds in which a test must finish in order to pass:

```
from nose.tools import timed

@timed(3)
def test_quick_function():
    assert_equal(quick_function(foo), "bar")
```

In the above example, the function call `quick_function(foo)` must not only return the correct answer, but must do so within three seconds.

A moment's thought will suggest a number of reasons why this type of test can be dangerous. A timed test that suddenly fails could indicate an inefficient change to the code – but it could equally well indicate that the test is being run on a slow computer, or on a fast computer that is under a heavy load. Use timed tests with care – for the vast majority of projects,

---

1 https://wiki.python.org/moin/PythonTestingToolsTaxonomy#GUI_Testing_Tools
2 https://wiki.python.org/moin/PythonTestingToolsTaxonomy#Web_Testing_Tools

profiling and benchmarking (as described in the chapter on performance) will be more useful tools for assessing speed.

Test-driven development and continuous integration testing

Two ideas that have gained ground recently involve approaches to software development which give testing an even more prominent role. In test-driven development (often abbreviated as TDD) the idea is to write the tests for a piece of software first, then start to write the code. As we've seen in the examples at the start of the chapter, one of the benefits of writing tests is that it forces you to think carefully about the behaviour that you want from your code.

The motivation behind test-driven development is that writing tests first will give us a clearer idea of what we are trying to achieve with a function (or method, class, etc.) which will lead to better focus and simpler designs for the code which we eventually produce.

Test-driven development can be carried out perfectly well using nose tests, so no additional tools are required. The nature of test-driven development means that it's most suitable for projects where the desired behaviour of the code is known (or at least can be easily figured out) at the start. For many scientific programming projects, this is not true – often we are writing code to explore potential solutions to a problem – and so test-driven development might not be a good fit.

Another technique that places heavy emphasis on testing is *continuous integration*: the practice of automatically testing changes to code and frequently integrating changes that pass the tests into the main code base. Continuous integration is closely tied to the idea of using version control and represents a tight coupling between the version control software and the testing framework that a development team is using. It tends to be most useful in the context of large, distributed teams working on large, mature software projects. Several tools are suitable for developing Python software using continuous integration[1], though they tend to involve a fair amount of overhead to set up.

Recap

In this chapter, we've seen how automated testing is really just a formalized way of carrying out the kind of checks that we often run on our code while we're writing it. With automated testing, rather than running a piece of code and manually checking the result we build a test suite that can do the job automatically and in a repeatable way. As we've seen, the benefits of automated testing include clearer thinking about the behaviour of our code, the ability to rapidly find new and reintroduced bugs, and greater confidence about the correct behaviour of our code.

If you are just getting started with automated testing, nose (which we discussed in detail earlier in the chapter) is a great choice. The tools described above will take care of testing for the vast majority of scientific software projects.

Conversely, if you are starting to contribute to a project that uses a different testing framework, or find that eventually you have to move on from nose, the concepts outlined in this chapter will still be very relevant. The ideas behind unit tests, fixtures, set up and tear-down methods, and mocking are common to all testing tools.

For projects that are just getting started, or for very small programs, it might seem that testing is too much of an overhead to bother with. Remember, though, that your approach to testing can evolve along with

---

[1] http://docs.python-guide.org/en/latest/scenarios/ci/

your code. You might start off with a handful of `assert()` statements at various points in your program, then collect them together into a testing script, then rewrite them to use `nose`, then split them into multiple test files for different parts of the program, etc. With experience, you will learn how best to divide your effort between writing new code and testing it.

5: Performance

Introduction

If you've read *Python for biologists* or *Advanced Python for Biologists*, you may have noticed that the topic of how to make code run quickly hardly ever comes up. That's deliberate; when learning how to use a programming language it's far more important to write **clear** code than fast code. However, when it comes to writing programs for the real world, performance becomes an issue. It can't have escaped anyone's notice that datasets in biology are large, and are only going to get larger.

In general, having programs that give you an answer quickly is better than having ones that give you an answer slowly. Since so much of modern scientific research involves exploring and investigating large datasets, it's very valuable to have a short turn around time between thinking of a question and getting an answer.

When talking about performance, there are a couple of aspects which might be important to us as scientists. The absolute speed of a program is one obvious one: given a particular dataset, how long does it take for our program to run? However, there are other, more subtle measurements that also matter. How does the time taken to run the program vary with the size of the dataset? How does the time taken change depending on the computer hardware we're using? And what is the relationship between the speed of a program and the amount of memory it uses?

In this chapter, we'll start by looking at a topic whose importance shouldn't need to be emphasized to anyone with a scientific background: **measuring**. Without being able to measure the execution time of our code, improving performance is nearly impossible – we need to be able to identify which parts of the code are slow, and to judge the effect of any changes we make. We'll look at two broad types of measurement: *benchmarking* (measuring how long a bit of code takes to run) and *profiling* (measuring which parts of a program take the most time). In this section we'll also take a brief look at the relationship between time and memory.

The second part of the chapter covers practical strategies and tools for making code run faster and more efficiently. We'll see the crucial role that data structures play in determining code performance and look at some common errors that result in slow code.

It's important to remember that measurements obtained by benchmarking and profiling depend on many factors: hardware, operating system, Python versions and system load can all have an effect. If you run any of the code samples in this chapter, you may well get different results to those printed in the text.

To end this introduction, a word of warning: performance optimization can be a fun and fascinating area of programming, but it's easy to get caught up in it at the expense of other things. Before diving in to start optimizing a piece of code, do a quick mental calculation to figure out how much time you're really going to save. If you have a program that you use few times a week and that takes a couple of minutes to run, spending a entire day getting the time down to a couple of seconds is unlikely to be a good investment of your time!

Benchmarking

Unix time

Let's start with the simplest question we can ask about our program's performance: how long does it take to run? If we happen to be on a Linux or Mac system, we can get an answer by prefixing our Python command with the `time` command:

```
$ time python myprogram.py

real    0m0.490s
user    0m0.457s
sys 0m0.032s
```

As we can see from the output, we get three measurements: *real*, *user* and *sys*. *Real* time is the time that we would measure on a clock – the amount of time that the program was running. This measurement isn't quite as useful as it seems though; our program will take longer to run on a busy system than on an idle one, so the real time may overestimate the running time of our program. A more useful measurement is the *user* time, which measures the amount of time our program was actually being executed by the CPU. This is a more useful measurement, because it doesn't include time that the computer spent running other programs.

Sys time (sort for system time) is the amount of time that our program spent waiting for the operating system to do something for it[1]. Adding together the user time and the sys time gives us the total time that was actually spent making the program work, and is probably the most accurate measurement of the "true" execution time of our program.

Manual timing

What if we need a more general tool for timing? An obvious solution is to just get the current time at the start of the program, then again at the end, and calculate the difference between the two. For historical reasons, in Python we measure time as the number of seconds since midnight January 1st 1970. We call that date the *epoch*, so if you look at the documentation

---

[1] Like opening files, allocating memory, or accessing the network – all the stuff that we don't normally worry about when writing Python code.

for the `time()` function in the `time` module you'll see that it returns the number of seconds since the start of the epoch. For this example we don't really care about when we count from, we only care about the relative time at the start and the end, so we can just subtract the end time from the start time to get the execution time in seconds:

```
import time
start = time.time()

# print the sum of the first million cube numbers
x = 0
for i in range(1000000):
    x = x + i ** 3
print(x)

end = time.time()
print(end - start)
```

manual_timing.py

```
249999500000250000000000
0.455631971359
```

As we can see from the second line of output this works fine, but it's subject to the same problem as the real time measured by the Unix `time` command: it's affected by the other processes on the system. For some situations this won't matter, but for most performance tuning problems it's better to use a more sophisticated solution.

The `timeit` module

Python comes with a built in module called `timeit` whose job is to carry out the kind of timing that we've been discussing above. It's been designed to make it as easy as possible to time the execution of small bits of code. The simplest way to use it is on the command line: use the option

Chapter 5:Performance

`-m timeit` to load the module, then supply the bit of code you want to time as the last command line argument. For example, let's use `timeit` to see how long it takes Python to carry out a simple calculation: how many unique 10-base DNA sequences are there (in mathematical terms, what's four raised to the power ten)? Recall that in Python we use two asterisks to indicate a power calculation, so the command to run is:

```
$ python -m timeit "4 ** 10"
```

Notice how the bit of code we want to execute is the last command line argument, and is enclosed in quotes. Now let's look at the output we get:

```
10000000 loops, best of 3: 0.031 usec per loop
```

We can see that `timeit` has done a number of helpful things. Firstly, it's figured out that because the bit of code we're testing is very small we should test it by running it lots of times (otherwise various types of overhead and noise will overwhelm the measurement). In this case, it's decided to run the bit of code ten million times in order to get an accurate measurement.

Secondly, it's repeated the whole test three times, in order to account for other processes that might be running at the same time. Notice that the final measurement that gets returned is the best (i.e. shortest) time, not the average time, since other processes can only ever increase the execution time.

Finally, it's reported the time in a unit we can easily understand (microseconds) with a sensible number of decimal places. A nice feature of `timeit` is that it will automatically adjust the number of loops and the measurement unit to take account of the code. See what happens if we time the execution of a more complicated task – checking to see if a given number is in a list of a million numbers[1]:

---

1   The example here is run under Python 2; it's several orders of magnitude faster in Python 3

Chapter 5:Performance

```
$ python -m timeit "12345 in range(1000000)"
```

```
10 loops, best of 3: 32.6 msec per loop
```

Because each iteration of this code takes much longer, it only gets run ten times per trial, and the answer is reported in milliseconds rather than microseconds.

If we think about the code in this second example, we realize that there are actually two separate things going on. First the `range()` function has to create the list of one million numbers, then Python can check each element to see if it's equal to 12345. Knowing this, we might suspect that the majority of the execution time is spent constructing the list rather than checking it. If this is the case, then our measurement of 32 milliseconds is mostly a measurement of how long it takes Python to create a list. How might we test this idea? One way to do it would be to run a timing test using code that just creates the list:

```
$ python -m timeit "range(1000000)"
```

```
10 loops, best of 3: 31 msec per loop
```

This confirms our suspicions: just constructing the list takes nearly as long as constructing it **and** then checking it. Another test we could do is to separate out the construction of the list from the checking of the list. We can do this by passing a `-s` (short for *setup*) command to `timeit` which contains the code to run before the test starts. Here's what it looks like:

```
$ python -m timeit -s "r=range(1000000)" "12345 in r"
```

```
1000 loops, best of 3: 155 usec per loop
```

In the setup code (the bit that comes after `-s`) we use `range()` to create a list then assign that list to the variable name `r`. Then, in the code we actually want to test, we check to see if the number 12345 is in the list `r`. In

---

because of improvements to the `range()` function.

Chapter 5:Performance

this version of the test Python creates the list once, then checks to see if 12345 is in the list many times. The time taken to create the list isn't included in the final result, so this version measures just the bit of code we're interested in. As we suspected, when we just look at the time required to check the list rather than build it, we get a much shorter execution time.

The command line version of `timeit` is very useful for short snippets of code, but what about timing larger blocks? We can use the setup code trick to import a function that we want to time. For example, if we take our cube-summing code from before, wrap it in a function, and save it in a file called `cubes.py`:

```python
def sum_cubes():
    x = 0
    for i in range(1000000):
        x = x + i ** 3
    return(x)
```
cubes.py

We can time the function by treating `cubes.py` as a module and importing it in the setup code for `timeit`[1], then calling the function in the test code:

```
$ python -m timeit -s "import cubes" "cubes.sum_cubes()"

10 loops, best of 3: 250 msec per loop
```

This technique allows us to quickly test the relative speed of different ways of solving a problem. For example, here's a short Python program that defines two different functions for calculating the AT content of a DNA

---

[1] For a detailed explanation of what's going on here, see the chapter on organizing and distributing code..

sequence, along with a short sequence for testing and an `assert` statement to confirm that they both give the same answer[1]:

```
from __future__ import division

def at_count(dna):
    return (dna.count('a') + dna.count('t')) / len(dna)

def at_iter(dna):
    a_count = 0
    t_count = 0
    for base in dna:
        if base == 'a':
            a_count = a_count + 1
        elif base == 't':
            t_count = t_count + 1
    return (a_count + t_count) / len(dna)


test_dna = 'atcgatcgatcatgatcggatcgtagctagcatctagtc'
assert(at_count(test_dna) == at_iter(test_dna))
```
at.py

The `at_count()` function uses the built in string `count()` method to count the A and T bases, whereas the `at_content_iter()` function iterates over the DNA sequence and updates the count whenever it sees A or T. Which function do we expect to be faster? The first function has to iterate over the DNA sequence twice (once for each `dna.count()` function call) whereas the second one counts both A and T in a single pass, so we might expect the second function to run faster. However, the timing results tell a different story:

```
$ python -m timeit -s "import at" "at.at_count(at.dna)"

1000000 loops, best of 3: 1 usec per loop

$ python -m timeit -s "import at" "at.at_iter(at.dna)"
```

---
1 See the chapter on testing for much more on `assert` statements.

Chapter 5:Performance

```
100000 loops, best of 3: 6.46 usec per loop
```

The function that uses iteration is actually several times slower even though it requires twice as many passes over the data[1].

We can also use the `timeit` module directly from within a Python program:

```
import timeit
print(timeit.timeit("12345 in range(1000000)", number=10))
```

but as we can see from the output:

```
0.347445964813
```

it's far less convenient – we miss out on the nice features like automatically figuring out the correct number of iterations, getting the best score out of three, and presenting the result in an easy-to-read format.

Benchmarking memory

Measuring memory usage turns out to be surprisingly tricky. Modern operating systems manage memory in various sophisticated ways, there are a number of different ways of measuring memory, and memory usage can vary wildly across the different stages of a program. Just as with timing, we'll consider a few different ways to measure memory usage.

The `resource` module

If you're running on a Linux or Mac system, then the `resource` module contains methods that will let you figure out how much memory a program is using. Calculating memory usage with the `resource` module involves a

---

[1] The underlying reason for this is that the loops in the `count()` method of the `string` class are implemented in C, which is much faster than the equivalent `for` loop in Python.

Chapter 5:Performance

few steps. First we call the `getrusage()` function with `resource.RUSAGE_SELF` as its argument (to indicate that we are interested in the memory usage of the currently running program). The output from `getrusage()` is an object with a number of fields corresponding to different measurements; the one we are interested in is called `ru_maxrss`. The code looks something like this:

```
from __future__ import division
import resource

resource_object = resource.getrusage(resource.RUSAGE_SELF)
memory = resource_object.ru_maxrss

print("Used this much memory: " + str(memory))
```

Confusingly, the units are different on different systems: on Linux the answer will be in kilobytes but on a Mac the answer will be in bytes. If we run the program as written above, we can see that to just run a Python program that does nothing requires about 5 megabytes on my computer:

```
Used this much memory: 5524
```

If we do something more interesting, like create a list of the first million integers, the memory usage goes up to around 40 megabytes:

```
from __future__ import division
import resource

r = range(1000000)

resource_object = resource.getrusage(resource.RUSAGE_SELF)
memory = resource_object.ru_maxrss

print("Used this much memory: " + str(memory))
```

measure_memory_resource.py

Chapter 5:Performance

```
Used this much memory: 37256
```

Using the `resource` module has many drawbacks: it's awkward to use, it only tracks increases in memory (i.e. there's no way to tell when memory is freed), it works differently on Linux and Mac systems, and it doesn't work at all on Windows systems. The one thing that it does have in its favour is that it's part of the Python standard library.

Getting memory information with `psutil`

One of the attractions of Python as a programming language is that, for any given problem, there's probably a module somewhere that will help us solve it, and measuring memory usage is no exception. `psutil` is a Python module that contains functions for getting information – including memory usage – about running processes. To use it, first make sure it's installed. Running

```
$ pip install psutil
```

will do the job on most systems.

The `psutil` module is designed to be able to get information about **any** running process, not just Python, so we need a way of specifying the process we're interested in. The way that we do that is to tell `psutil` the *process id*. The *process id* is simply a label that the operating system uses to identify a running process. Within a Python program, we can find the process id by calling the `getpid()` function in the `os` module:

```
import os
my_pid = os.getpid()
```

Once we have the process id, we can construct a new `Process` object:

```
import psutil
my_process = psutil.Process(my_pid)
```

and then ask the `Process` object for its memory usage:

```
mem = process.get_memory_info()
```

If we simply print the value of `mem`, we'll see that it is an object with two fields: `rss` and `vms`. For memory benchmarking, `rss` is the most useful measurement, so normally we just grab the `rss` field. Because `psutil` gives an answer in bytes, we'll divide by 1000 to get a measurement in kilobytes[1]. When we put these steps together, the code looks like this:

```
import psutil, os

process = psutil.Process(os.getpid())
mem = process.get_memory_info().rss / 1000
print("Used this much memory: " + str(mem))
```

```
Used this much memory: 7802
```

Notice how importing the `psutil` module has increased the baseline memory usage to just under 8 megabytes. If we repeat our earlier experiment and measure the memory usage after creating a list of a million elements:

```
import psutil, os

r = range(1000000)

process = psutil.Process(os.getpid())
mem = process.memory_info().rss / 1000
print("Used this much memory: " + str(mem))
```

---

[1] For this example, a kilobyte is one thousand bytes. In some contexts, a kilobyte is $2^{10} = 1024$ bytes.

Chapter 5:Performance

measure_memory_psutil.py

We find that, just like before, we use around 40 megabytes of memory:

```
Used this much memory: 40312
```

`psutil` has several advantages over `resource`. Not only does it work on all different systems, but it behaves identically on each. We can also use it to examine what happens to memory as a program is running. Here's a program that executes three statements:

1. create a variable to store a list of half a million even numbers
2. discard that list by reassigning the variable to an empty list
3. assign the variable to a list of half a million odd numbers

and prints memory usage before and after each step:

Chapter 5:Performance

```
import psutil, os

def print_mem():
    process = psutil.Process(os.getpid())
    mem = process.memory_info().rss / 1000
    print("Used this much memory: " + str(mem))

print("before creating list one...")
print_mem()

r = range(0, 1000000, 2)

print("after creating list one...")
print_mem()

r = []

print("after discarding list one...")
print_mem()

r = range(1, 1000000, 2)

print("after creating list two...")
print_mem()
```

running_memory.py

Looking at the output reveals some interesting patterns:

```
before creating list one...
Used this much memory: 7811

after creating list one...
Used this much memory: 24031

after discarding list one...
Used this much memory: 20029

after creating list two...
Used this much memory: 24027
```

Before the first list is created, the program is using just under 8 megabytes, as expected. After creating the first list of half a million elements, the

Chapter 5:Performance

memory usage jumps to 24 megabytes. After discarding this first list, the memory usage goes down, but not by as much as we might expect: instead of dropping back down to 8 megabytes it drops to 20 megabytes. Clearly, Python is holding onto some of the extra memory even though it doesn't need it. Finally, after creating the second list, the memory usage goes back up to 24 megabytes: Python has recycled some of the memory that it previously used for the first list[1].

Time and memory trade-offs

Equipped with the tools to measure CPU time and memory usage, we can begin to investigate the trade-offs involved in program design. Let's return to our big list example: a program that creates a list of a million numbers then checks to see if one particular number is in that list. Recall from earlier in the chapter that with a list of a million numbers and the target number 12345 it took about 150 microseconds to check the number:

```
$ python -m timeit -s "r=range(1000000)" "12345 in r"
1000 loops, best of 3: 155 usec per loop
```

If we put the code inside a Python file:

```
l = range(1000000)

def number_in_list():
    return 12345 in l
```

big_list.py

then we can use the setup argument to `timeit` to import it like we did before:

---

1   This is a drastic over-simplification of how memory management actually works in Python!

Chapter 5:Performance

```
$ python -m timeit -s "import big_list" "big_list.number_in_list()"
1000 loops, best of 3: 205 usec per loop
```

This time it takes a bit longer, because we've got the extra overhead of calling a function each time.

We can now modify the code to print the memory usage after creating the list – we just add the definition for the `print_mem()` function that we saw earlier and call it right after the list has been created:

```
import psutil, os

def print_mem():
    process = psutil.Process(os.getpid())
    mem = process.memory_info().rss / 1000
    print("Used this much memory: " + str(mem))

l = range(1000000)
print_mem()

def number_in_list():
    return 12345 in l
```

big_list_memory.py

Now we can get the memory information:

```
$ python big_list_memory.py
Used this much memory: 40710
```

As we might have expected from our previous experiments, the memory usage is around 40 megabytes.

How might we try to speed this program up? Intuitively, it seems obvious that in order to check whether a given number is in a list we need to check each element of the list, which is likely to be slow. Maybe it would be faster if we used a set instead of a list? Let's find out – all we have to do is make a copy of the `big_list.py` code, change the list to a set and save it under a different name:

Chapter 5:Performance

```
import psutil, os

def print_mem():
    ...

s = set(range(1000000))
print_mem()

def number_in_set():
    return 12345 in s
```

big_set.py

When we run the `timeit` command line on this new file, the results are dramatic:

```
$ python -m timeit -s "import big_set" "big_set.number_in_set()"
Used this much memory: 66301
1000000 loops, best of 3: 0.278 usec per loop
```

The set takes up around 50% more memory than the list, but is around one thousand times faster.

From this point, there are a number of different questions we could explore. What happens if we change the number are looking for? Changing the function definition to look for the number one:

```
def number_in_list():
    return 1 in l

def number_in_set():
    return 1 in s
```

doesn't affect the timing for the set, but makes the list much faster – in fact it brings the timing down from ~200 microseconds to ~0.25 microseconds. This makes intuitive sense, since Python can stop looking at the elements of the list when it finds the number it's looking for and the number one is always going to be near the start of the list. The worst case scenario is checking the list for a number that isn't there:

155

```
def number_in_list():
    return -1 in l
```

which increases the timing to 20 milliseconds (20,000 microseconds or one hundred times slower than our original trial with the number 12345). In contrast, the choice of number makes no difference to the speed of the code that uses a set.

Let's investigate the effects of a different change: what happens to the timings when we change the number of elements in the list/set? To avoid having the calculations affected by the position effect we saw above, we'll change the code slightly and turn the number of elements into a variable. This will allow us to easily pick a number from the middle of the list as the one we're searching for. The code for the list now looks like this:

```
import psutil, os

def print_mem():
    ...

size = 1000000

l = range(size)

# try to find a number that's halfway
target = size/2

print_mem()

def number_in_list():
    return target in l
```

big_list_variable.py

By varying the `size` parameter, we can see how the timing changes with the number of elements in the list. As we might expect, the time increases roughly linearly with the number of elements: for one million elements each test takes ~9 milliseconds, for ten million each test takes ~90 milliseconds, and for one hundred million each test takes ~900 milliseconds. The memory usage increases roughly linearly as well (if we take into account a constant ~10 megabyte overhead) from ~40 megabytes to ~300 megabytes to ~3000 megabytes.

Now let's look at the same series of sizes for the code which uses a set:

```
import psutil, os

def print_mem():
    ...

size = 1000000
s = set(range(size))
target = size/2
print_mem()

def number_in_set():
    return target in s
```

big_set_variable.py

The behaviour of the set code is very different. As we increase the size from one million to ten million to one hundred million elements, the memory usage goes up more or less linearly, from ~60 megabytes to ~600 megabytes to ~6000 megabytes. However, the time doesn't change at all – it stays constant around ~0.2 microseconds.

There's a convenient shorthand for talking about how operations on datasets – in this case, checking for inclusion – vary with the size. It's called *big O notation*. To describe the behaviour of an operation we just write an upper case O followed by the relationship of the running time to the variable **n**, which represents the size of the input. In the case of our list example, we would say that checking to see if an element is in a list is **O(n)**, which means that the time increases linearly with the number of elements. For the set example, the time doesn't increase at all, which we represent as **O(1)** – the variable n (which represents the size) is left out, because it doesn't affect the running time. If we had an operation where the time increased with the square of the size (anything involving pairwise comparisons generally falls into this category), we would write **O(n^2)**. You'll often see big O notation used in documentation to describe how operations on data structures scale with their size.

Before we leave this example, let's try one more experiment. So far we've deliberately set up the timing tests so that the time taken to create the set or list is **not** included in the results. In other words, we're simulating a situation where we want to create a single list or set and then check many different numbers against it. As we've seen, in this situation a set gives a massive speed improvement over a list with only a modest increase in the amount of memory required. However, what happens in a situation where we only want to check a single number against a given set or list? We can get the answer using a `timeit` command. Creating a list of one million elements and then checking to see if a number is in it takes around 50 milliseconds on my system:

```
$ python -m timeit "500000 in range(1000000)"

10 loops, best of 3: 47.9 msec per loop
```

Whereas doing the same with a set takes over twice as long:

```
$ python -m timeit "500000 in set(range(1000000))"

10 loops, best of 3: 120 msec per loop
```

From this series of experiments on sets and lists we can get an idea of how they behave and start to come up with some rules for when to use each. For the specific case we've been looking at there – checking whether a number is in a large collection of numbers – sets are likely to be most useful as long as (1) we need to search for multiple numbers in the same collection of elements and (2) we have enough memory for the data we're interested in.

The fact that we're using `range()` to generate our list of numbers for this example suggests a much simpler way to test if a number is in the list: just check if it's less than the limit of the range – n fact, that's exactly how `range()` works in Python 3. A more realistic example would involve generating a list of random numbers, but that would make the examples harder to read.

Chapter 5:Performance

Profiling

So far in this chapter we've looked at tools for measuring several aspects of code performance: how long does a piece of code take to run? how much memory does it use? and how do these two things vary with the size of the data? As we've seen, these tools are very useful for investigating the behaviour of small bits of code. However, they're not terribly useful for solving the common performance challenge of taking a program and making it faster or more memory efficient. For any reasonably sized program there are likely to be many potential places where we could make improvements, but some of them will have a much greater impact on the overall running time of the program.

Let's look at a simple example. Imagine we have a single long DNA sequence and a collection of 4 base motifs that are interesting for some reason[1]. We want to to identify all of the frequently occurring 4 base chunks in the DNA sequence and divide them into two categories: those that are in our list of interesting motifs, and those that are not.

Here's one possible solution, assuming that our definition for a frequently occurring chunk of DNA is one that occurs more than 50 times:

---

1 Perhaps they are transcription factor binding motifs.

Chapter 5:Performance

```
dna = "ATCGTACGTACT..."
motifs = ["ATCG" , "ATCC" , ... , ...]

frequent_chunks = []
for start in range(len(dna) - 3):     ❶
    chunk = dna[start:start + 4]      ❷
    if dna.count(chunk) > 50:         ❸
        frequent_chunks.append(chunk)

for chunk in frequent_chunks:
    if chunk in motifs:               ❹
        print(chunk + " is frequent and interesting")
    else:
        print(chunk + " is frequent but not interesting")
```

chunks.py

The logic here is pretty straightforward[1]. First, we iterate over each overlapping 4 base chunk of the DNA sequence❶ and store it in the variable `chunk`❷. We then count the number of times that particular chunk appears in the DNA sequence and, if it appears more than 50 times, add the chunk to the list of frequently occurring chunks. Next we iterate over the list of frequently occurring chunks and, for each one, ask whether it's in the list of motifs we are looking for❹ and print a message saying whether is in the interesting list or not.

Note: I've presented the code here as if we were hard coding the DNA sequence and the list of motifs: in the real world, we would probably want to read them from a file. The example file contains code to randomly generate DNA sequence and lists of motifs so that you can experiment with different parameters if you like. Also note that this is a very similar program to the one we used to illustrate refactoring in the chapter on automated testing.

---

1   If you're already thinking that this is a terrible way to solve the problem, you're right... but it will do as an example.

With a ten kilobase DNA sequence and a list of 100 interesting motifs, this program takes ~450 milliseconds on my system:

```
$ python -m timeit -s "import chunks"

CGGT is frequent but not interesting
GGTG is frequent and interesting
GAAG is frequent but not interesting
...
100000000 loops, best of 3: 452 msec per loop
```

How might we speed it up? We learned in the previous section that checking whether whether a given element is in a list is slow. What happens if we change the list to a set? Making the change to the code is easy – we only have to change the line where we create the collection of motifs:

```
dna = "ATCGTACGTACT..."
motifs = set(["ATCG" , "ATCC" , ... , ...])

...
```

but the results are less than impressive: the execution time doesn't change at all. Why might that be? Looking back at the code, it seems likely that the line where we check if a frequently occurring chunk is in the list of interesting motifs❹ doesn't actually get run very often. In fact, if we add a line to print the length of the `frequent_chunks` list, we can see that there are around 400 elements, so that line will only get executed 400 times. Other lines get executed much more often, so maybe they have a bigger contribution to the overall execution time.

In order to concentrate our coding efforts where they can make the most improvement, we need a way of measuring the execution time for different sections of code. We call this *profiling*.

Chapter 5:Performance

Profiling with `cProfile`

Python's built in profiling tool is the `cProfile` module. Using it is very straightforward: we just import the module then call its `run()` function giving the code we want to run as a string argument. To make this work for our program, we need to wrap the code in a function first:

```
import cProfile

dna = "ATCGTACGTACT..."
motifs = set(["ATCG" , "ATCC" , ... , ...])

def classify_chunks():
    frequent_chunks = []
    for start in range(len(dna) - 3):
        chunk = dna[start:start + 4]
        if dna.count(chunk) > 50:
            frequent_chunks.append(chunk)

    for chunk in frequent_chunks:
        if chunk in motifs:
            print(chunk + " is frequent and interesting")
        else:
            print(chunk + " is frequent but not interesting")

cProfile.run("classify_chunks()")
```

When we run this code, in addition to the normal output we get some output from `cProfile` (reformatted slightly to make it fit on the page better):

```
         10422 function calls in 0.620 seconds

   Ordered by: standard name

   ncalls  tottime  percall  cumtime  percall filename:lineno(function)
        1    0.000    0.000    0.620    0.620 <string>:1(<module>)
        1    0.009    0.009    0.620    0.620 ...(classify_chunks)
        2    0.000    0.000    0.000    0.000 {len}
      419    0.000    0.000    0.000    0.000 {method 'append' of 'list' objects}
     9997    0.612    0.000    0.612    0.000 {method 'count' of 'str' objects}
        1    0.000    0.000    0.000    0.000 {range}
```

The first line of output tells us that the code took 0.62 seconds to run, and that `cProfile` measured 10422 function calls in that time. Note that running the code with `cProfile` is slightly slower due to the overhead of measurement – before it only took 0.45 seconds.

The main body of the output is in tabular format. Each row contains information about a particular function or method, and contains a number of columns. The columns are, from left to right:

- *ncalls*, which tells us how many times the function was called

- *tottime*, which tells us the total amount of time that was spent in that function (not including subfunctions)

- *percall*, which tells us the amount of time that was spent in that function (**not** including subfunctions) each time it was called

- *cumtime*, which is like *tottime* but **does** include subfunctions

- another *percall*, which is like the first one except that it does include subfunctions

- *filename:lineno(function)*, which tells us the filename, line number, and name of the function or method

Chapter 5:Performance

That's a lot of information! Let's take a look at a few specific rows to see if we can interpret what's going on. Here's the row for the function `classify_chunks()`:

```
ncalls tottime  percall  cumtime  percall filename:lineno(function)
   1    0.009    0.009    0.620    0.620   ...(classify_chunks)
```

As expected it's only called once. The *tottime*, which doesn't include subfunctions, is small – just 0.009 seconds. But the *cumtime*, which does include subfunctions, is 0.620 seconds. In other words, most of the running time for the program is spent in this function, but nearly all of that time is spent in other functions that are called from within it.

Next, here's the row for the `append()` method of `list` objects:

```
ncalls tottime  percall cumtime percall filename:lineno(function)
 419    0.000    0.000   0.000   0.000   {method 'append' of 'list' objects}
```

It's called 419 times, which makes sense, because the only time we call the `append()` function is when we have found a frequently occurring chunk, which happens around 400 times. But look at the rest of the columns; even with more than 400 calls, the amount of times the `append()` method takes is so small it gets rounded down to zero.

Finally, here's the row for the `count()` method of `string` objects:

```
ncalls tottime percall  cumtime  percall filename:lineno(function)
9997   0.612   0.000    0.612    0.000   {method 'count' of 'str' objects}
```

This method is called around 10000 times – once for each 4 base chunk in the DNA sequence. Just as with the `append()` method, the time taken for each individual function call (*percall*) is so small that it gets rounded down to zero. However, because the number of times this function is called is so large, the total time (or cumulative time; both are the same here) is 0.612 seconds – most of the execution time of the program.

Taken together, we can use these bits of information to infer something useful about the distribution of execution time in our program: the vast majority is taken up by counting the number of times each 4 base chunk occurs. This explains why changing motifs from a `list` to a `set` didn't affect the overall execution time.

Useful as `cProfile` is, it has a couple of severe limitations. If we take another look at the output, we can see that quite a lot of our code appears to have no timing information. Bits of code for extracting the chunk, checking if the count is greater than 50, and checking whether a chunk is in the collection of motifs are not represented anywhere in the table. The reason for this is that `cProfile` can **only** measure function and method calls. Statements like these:

```
chunk = dna[start:start + 4]
dna.count(chunk) > 50
chunk in motifs
```

don't include a function or method call and are thus invisible to `cProfile`. In contrast, ones like these:

```
classify_chunks()
range(len(dna)
dna.count(chunk)
frequent_chunks.append(chunk)
```

do include functions or methods and thus are measured. Because of this limitation, `cProfile` tends to work best in structured programs that are divided into multiple functions. Consider this version of the code in which the processes of finding frequently occurring chunks and comparing them

Chapter 5:Performance

to known motifs are written as separate functions (the code inside the functions is exactly the same as before):

```
import cProfile

dna = "ATCGTACGTACT..."
motifs = set(["ATCG" , "ATCC" , ... , ...])

def get_frequent_chunks(dna):
    frequent_chunks = []
    for start in range(len(dna) - 3):
        chunk = dna[start:start + 4]
        if dna.count(chunk) > 50:
            frequent_chunks.append(chunk)
    return frequent_chunks

def print_chunks(chunks):
    for chunk in chunks:
        if chunk in motifs:
            print(chunk + " is frequent and interesting")
        else:
            print(chunk + " is frequent but not interesting")

def classify_chunks():
    frequent_chunks = get_frequent_chunks(dna)
    print_chunks(frequent_chunks)

cProfile.run("classify_chunks()")
```

chunks_separate_functions.py

Now when we run the program and look at the relevant bit of the `cProfile` output:

Chapter 5:Performance

```
         10397 function calls in 0.624 seconds

   Ordered by: standard name

ncalls  tottime  percall   cumtime   percall  filename:lineno(function)
   1     0.005    0.005     0.619     0.619   (get_frequent_chunks)
   1     0.004    0.004     0.004     0.004   (print_chunks)
...
```

it's immediately obvious, looking at the *cumtime* column, that `get_frequent_chunks()` uses the vast majority of the time, and that if we want to speed up our program we should concentrate on that function first.

Another limitation of `cProfile` is that the output makes it difficult to distinguish between different calls to the same function or method. Here's a trivial example:

```
import cProfile

# long_dna has ten million characters
long_dna = "ATGCTG..."

# short_dna has one million characters
short_dna = "ATGCTG..."

def count_As():
    long_count = long_dna.count('A')
    short_count = short_dna.count('A')

cProfile.run("count_As()")
```

The `long_dna` variable is ten times longer than the `short_dna` variable, so the first `count()` method call will take ten times longer than the second one. When we look at the `cProfile` output, however:

Chapter 5:Performance

```
        5 function calls in 0.069 seconds
ncalls  tottime  percall  cumtime  percall filename:lineno(function)
     1    0.000    0.000    0.069    0.069 <string>:1(<module>)
     1    0.000    0.000    0.069    0.069 slowfast.py:15(count_As)
     2    0.069    0.035    0.069    0.035 {method 'count' of 'str' objects}
```

The time for the two `count()` method calls get aggregated together so there's no way to tell that one is actually ten times slower than the other.

Profiling with `line_profiler`

The `line_profiler` module[1] takes an entirely different approach to profiling. Rather than adding up the total time for each function call, it adds up the total time for each line of Python code, resulting in output that is much easier to interpret. Unlike `cProfile`, `line_profiler` isn't part of the standard distribution, so you'll have to install it yourself. Running

```
$ pip install line_profiler
```

will do the job on most systems.

Using `line_profiler` is simple. We use the `@profile` decorator to tell the module which function we want to profile – on our short/long DNA example it looks like this:

```
# long_dna has ten million characters
long_dna = "ATGCTG..."

 # short_dna has one million characters
short_dna = "ATGCTG..."

@profile
def count_As():
    long_count = long_dna.count('A')
    short_count = short_dna.count('A')

count_As()
```

---

1   https://github.com/rkern/line_profiler

Chapter 5:Performance

short_long_profile.py

To actually carry out the profiling, we use the `kernprof` command line tool (part of the `line_profiler` package). We use the `-l` option to indicate that we want line-by-line profiling, and the `-v` option to view the results. The command line looks like this:

```
$ kernprof -l -v short_long_profile.py
```

and the output looks like this:

```
Wrote profile results to short_long_profile.py.lprof
Timer unit: 1e-06 s

Total time: 0.05597 s
File: slowfast.py
Function: count_As at line 10

Line #   Hits    Time   Per Hit   % Time  Line Contents
==============================================================
    10                                    @profile
    11                                    def count_As():
    12    1     49976   49976.0    89.3     long_count = long_dna.count('A')
    13    1      5994    5994.0    10.7     short_count = short_dna.count('A')
```

Just like `cProfile`, the measurements are presented in rows and columns, but now each row represents a single line in the Python file. The columns, from left to right, give:

- the line number
- the number of times that the line was executed
- the total amount of time spent executing the line
- the amount of time to execute the line once
- the percentage of the total time spent executing the line

Chapter 5:Performance

On the far right of the output is the Python code itself. The output also shows the units for measurement (10^{-6} seconds i.e. microseconds), the total time, the name of the file and the name and position of the function.

Compared to `cProfile`, the output is much easier to interpret – for our example above it's easy to see that counting the number of As in the long DNA sequence occupies around 90% of the total time. Let's try it on the very first version of our chunk-finding code from the start of this section:

```
dna = "ATCGTACGTACT..."
motifs = ["ATCG" , "ATCC" , ... , ...]

@profile
def classify_chunks():
    frequent_chunks = []
    for start in range(len(dna) - 3):
        chunk = dna[start:start + 4]
        if dna.count(chunk) > 50:
            frequent_chunks.append(chunk)

    for chunk in frequent_chunks:
        if chunk in motifs:
            print(chunk + " is frequent and interesting")
        else:
            print(chunk + " is frequent but not interesting")

classify_chunks()
```

profile_chunks.py

The output shows statistics for every line and contains a lot of information – here's what it looks like, slightly reformatted to fit on the page:

Chapter 5:Performance

```
Timer unit: 1e-06 s

Total time: 0.651772 s
File: profile_chunks.py
Function: classify_chunks at line 12

Line Hits      Time  Per Hit   % Time  Line Contents
=============================================================
12                                     @profile
13                                     def classify_chunks():
14      1         2     2.0      0.0       frequent_chunks = []
15   9998      8375     0.8      1.3       for start in range(len(dna) - 3):
16   9997     10641     1.1      1.6           chunk = dna[start:start + 4]
17   9997    625270    62.5     95.9           if dna.count(chunk) > 50:
18    482       514     1.1      0.1               frequent_chunks.append(chunk)
19
20    483       753     1.6      0.1       for chunk in frequent_chunks:
21    482      1734     3.6      0.3           if chunk in motifs:
22     51       453     8.9      0.1               print(chunk + "...interesting")
23                                             else:
24    431      4030     9.4      0.6               print(chunk + "...not interesting")
```

Glancing at the *% Time* column we can see straight away that 95% of the total execution time is taken up counting the number of times that a particular chunk appears in the DNA sequence (line 17). The line that we tried to optimize earlier in the chapter – where we check if a frequently occurring chunk is in the list of interesting motifs (line 21) – takes up just 0.3% of the total time. This dramatically illustrates why our attempt to speed up the program by making this line faster was never going to work. No matter how fast we manage to make this line, we can never reduce the overall running time by more than a fraction of a percent.

Making use of profiling data

Having used a combination of `cProfile` and `line_profiler` to investigate the behaviour of our `classify_chunks()` function, we can now do a much more effective job of speeding it up. As we saw above, the

Chapter 5:Performance

vast majority of the execution time is taken up counting the number of times a particular 4 base chunk of DNA occurs:

```
dna.count(chunk)
```

so in order to make a significant speed-up, we need to find a way of counting the chunks that avoids using the `count()` method. Here's one way to do it: we'll use a dict❶ to keep a running total of the number of times we've seen each chunk. Just like before, we'll go through the DNA sequence one chunk at a time. For each chunk we'll look up the number of times we've seen it (with a default of zero)❷, increase the count by one, and store the new value back in the dict❸. After counting all the chunks, we iterate over the items in the dict❹ and process just the chunks with a count of at least 50:

```
def classify_chunks():
    chunk_count = {} ❶
    for start in range(len(dna) - 3):
        chunk = dna[start:start + 4]
        current_count = chunk_count.get(chunk, 0) ❷
        new_count = current_count + 1
        chunk_count[chunk] = new_count ❸

    for chunk, count in chunk_count.items(): ❹
        if count > 50:
            if chunk in motifs:
                print(chunk + " is frequent and interesting")
            else:
                print(chunk + " is frequent but not interesting")
```

profile_chunks_dict.py

This is exactly the same approach we used when counting common kmers in the chapter on testing.

Chapter 5:Performance

What effect does this have on the performance of the code? By running the `kernprof` command again, we can get the answer (again, reformatted slightly to be easier to read):

```
Timer unit: 1e-06 s

Total time: 0.055759 s
File: chunks.py
Function: classify_chunks at line 16

Line #  Hits  Time  Per Hit %Time  Line Contents
==============================================================
    16                                @profile
    17                                def classify_chunks():
    18      1      2   2.0    0.0    chunk_count = {}
    19   9998    638   1.0   17.3    for start in range(len(dna) - 3):
    20   9997  11714   1.2   21.0        chunk = dna[start:start + 4]
    21   9997  13009   1.3   23.3        current_count = chunk_count.get(chunk, 0)
    22   9997   9784   1.0   17.5        new_count = current_count + 1
    23   9997  10589   1.1   19.0        chunk_count[chunk] = new_count
    24
    25
    26    257    299   1.2    0.5    for chunk, count in chunk_count.items():
    27    256    243   0.9    0.4        if count > 50:
    28     11     40   3.6    0.1            if chunk in motifs:
    29      3    106  35.3    0.2                print(chunk + " is ... interesting ")
    30                                        else:
    31      8    335  41.9    0.6                print(chunk + " is ... not interesting")
```

Several interesting differences stand out. Most strikingly, the total time has reduced by a factor of ten – the original code took 0.65 seconds, the new code took 0.05 seconds.

If we look at the *% Time* column, we can also see that the time isn't dominated by a single line as it was before. In the new code, lines 19 to 23 – the lines responsible for iterating over start positions, extracting the chunk, looking up the count, calculating the new count, and storing the new count – each take up around 20% of the total run time.

Chapter 5:Performance

This has important implications for any further attempts to speed up the program: we are not going to be able to get another big improvement just by changing a single line. Any further improvements are likely to come from making small adjustments. For example, we don't really need to create a new variable to hold the new count – we could replace this:

```
current_count = chunk_count.get(chunk, 0)
new_count = current_count + 1
chunk_count[chunk] = new_count
```

with this:

```
current_count = chunk_count.get(chunk, 0)
chunk_count[chunk] = current_count + 1
```

which brings the execution time down to 0.045 seconds.

By the same logic, we don't even need the `current_count` variable – we can look up the current count, increment it, and store the updated count in a single statement:

```
chunk_count[chunk] = chunk_count.get(chunk, 0) + 1
```

bringing the execution time down to 0.037 seconds.

Profiling with realistic data

For many pieces of code, profiling results are sensitive to the inputs. In other words, the relative time taken to execute different statements can be affected by the data that the code is working on.

Here's a concrete example. Imagine we have a function that calculates the AT content of a DNA sequence:

Chapter 5:Performance

```
def at_content(dna):
    return (dna.count('A') + dna.count('T')) / len(dna)
```

and another function that tests whether or not two DNA sequences have the same first five bases:

```
def same_start(dna1, dna2):
    return dna1[0:5] == dna2[0:5]
```

Now suppose that we have a large collection of DNA sequences, and we want to identify sequences that:

- have an AT content greater than some cutoff, and
- share their first five bases with at least one other sequence

Here's how we might go about identifying such sequences:

```
def find_interesting(dnas, cutoff):
    interesting = set() ❶
    for one in dnas:
        at = at_content(one)
        if at > cutoff:
            for two in dnas: ❷
                if one != two and same_start(one, two): ❸
                    interesting.add(one) ❹

    return(interesting)
```

find_interesting_seqs.py

In this function, we create an empty set to hold the interesting sequences❶. We then iterate over the list of sequences and calculate the AT content for each. If the AT content is greater than the cutoff, we iterate again over the list of sequences❷, checking every other sequence to see if it shares the first five bases with our current sequence❸. As soon as we find a non-identical sequence that shares the first five bases, we add our current sequence to the interesting set❹.

Chapter 5:Performance

Which function – `at_content()` or `same_start()` – do we expect to take the most time when we run this code? It's hard to tell just by looking at the code. We might guess that `at_content()` will be slower to execute because it involves looking at the whole sequence rather than just the first five bases. However, we might also guess that `same_start()` will be called more often, because we have to compare each pair of sequences.

Instead of guessing, let's reach for our profiling tools. Creating a list of 1000 DNA sequences, each 1000 bases long[1], and setting the cutoff to 0.545 yields the following output from `line_profiler`:

```
Timer unit: 1e-06 s

Total time: 0.022617 s
File: real_data.py
Function: find_interesting at line 15

#   Hits    Time    PerHit  %Time   Line Contents
==============================================================
15                                  @profile
16                                  def find_interesting(dnas, cutoff):
17    1       4       4.0     0.0     interesting = set()
18    1001    712     0.7     3.1     for one in dnas:
19    1000    15759   15.8    69.7      at = at_content(one)
20    1000    798     0.8     3.5       if at > cutoff:
21    2002    1435    0.7     6.3         for two in dnas:
22    2000    3898    1.9     17.2          if one != two and same_start(one, two):
23    3       10      3.3     0.0             interesting.add(one)
24
25    1       1       1.0     0.0     return(interesting)
```

Remember that the DNA sequences are randomly generated, so if you try this yourself you'll get different results.

Looking at this output, it seems obvious that the `at_content()` function is the slowest part of the code, taking 70% of the run time of the program.

---

1   The code to do this is in the examples file, if you want to experiment with it.

However, look what happens if we try a bigger dataset: here's the results from the exact same code using a list of 10,000 DNA sequences:

```
#   Hits   Time    Per Hit  %Time  Line Contents
================================================================
15                                 @profile
16                                 def find_interesting(dnas, cutoff):
17      1       8   8.0    0.0      interesting = set()
18  10001    5258   0.5    0.9      for one in dnas:
19  10000  115145  11.5   20.2          at = at_content(one)
20  10000    6778   0.7    1.2          if at > cutoff:
21 210021  127279   0.6   22.4              for two in dnas:
22 210000  314359   1.5   55.2                  if one != two and same_start(one, two):
23    207     265   1.3    0.0                      interesting.add(one)
24
25      1       1   1.0    0.0      return(interesting)
```

The allocation of time has changed dramatically; now the `same_start()` function is taking the most time. The reason for this behaviour is that `same_start()` is called in the inner loop, so the number of times it's called will increase with the square of the size of the dataset, whereas `at_content()` is called in the outer loop, so the number of times it's called will increase linearly with the size of the dataset. In terms of the big O notation we saw earlier, the part of the code where `at_content()` is called is **O(N)**, whereas the part of the code where `same_start()` is called is **O(N²)**.

We get a similar effect if we keep the dataset at its original size of 1000 sequences, but decrease the AT content cutoff so that more sequences pass it. With a cutoff of 0.525 we get a much higher proportion of time used by `same_start()`:

Chapter 5:Performance

```
#   Hits    Time  PerHit %Time Line Contents
==============================================================
15                                 @profile
16                                 def find_interesting(dnas, cutoff):
17      1      3    3.0   0.0     interesting = set()
18   1001    515    0.5   0.4     for one in dnas:
19   1000  11464   11.5   9.2         at = at_content(one)
20   1000    671    0.7   0.5         if at > cutoff:
21  56056  30094    0.5  24.1             for two in dnas:
22  56000  82149    1.5  65.7                 if one != two and same_start(one, two):
23     55    133    2.4   0.1                     interesting.add(one)
24
25      1      1    1.0   0.0     return(interesting)
```

Notice that in both these cases – increasing the number of DNA sequences and decreasing the AT content cutoff – the code has remained **exactly the same**. This has important implications for performance tuning. As we saw earlier, if we want to make our code faster we should concentrate on the slowest part, but for this example, the slowest part will change depending on what type of data we expect to be analysing. If we intend to use this program in the real world on smaller datasets with strict AT cutoff values then we should try to improve the `at_content()` function. Conversely, if we intend to use it on larger datasets with less strict AT cutoff values then we should try to improve the `same_start()` function[1].

Guidelines for performance optimization

Now that we've looked at the various tools available, we can begin to lay out a general strategy for improving the performance of a Python program.

The first step is always to carefully consider whether the current performance is good enough. Use `timeit` to benchmark your program on a range of different inputs and try to get an idea of how the running time

---

[1] In actual fact, both the functions are so simple that editing them is unlikely to yield much improvement – I have kept them deliberately simple to serve as examples.

varies. A useful exercise can be to try running your program on different size datasets and plotting the execution time on a chart. If you double the size of your dataset, does the execution time stay the same, or does it increase linearly or exponentially? What effect will this have on your work? If your program is already fast enough on realistic size datasets, then it may be that the time you would have to spend improving it could be better spent doing something else.

If you decide that you do need your program to run faster, start by using `cProfile` to look at the distribution of run time over functions. If your program isn't already divided into logical functions, then it's probably a good idea to fix this first before attempting any profiling. Eventually you are going to want to start refactoring the code, which will be a lot easier if it's well structured to begin with.

From the `cProfile` output you should be able to see if there's a particular function which is responsible for a big chunk of execution time. Looking in more detail at the output will tell you more why that is. Does the function execute quickly, but is called many times, leading to a large overall time? If so, look at the surrounding code that calls the function – it may be possible to reduce the number of times the function is called, especially if it's involved in a loop. Alternatively, is the function called a small number of times, but each individual call is slow? If so then it's going to be necessary to look inside the function using `line_profiler`.

Whichever tool you use, your profiling results will show you which parts of the code are responsible for the most execution time. Now begins the process of rewriting the slow parts of the code to speed them up. It's impossible to give general guidelines for this as there are so many things that can result in slow code (though see the next section for some ideas). For many problems, speeding up the code might involve a very different approach – look back to our example where we switched from counting individual chunks of DNA to assembling a dict of counts in a single pass.

Whatever changes you end up making to your code, there are a few important rules to follow. Once you've made a change, benchmark your code again to see if it's actually faster, and profile your code again to see where the new slow parts are. Remember to benchmark and profile with realistic data. If the code you're working on is actually being used for real work, then it's a **very** good idea to make use of automated testing – as described in the testing chapter – to make sure that your improvements to the code don't change its behaviour.

Specific tips for improving performance

Given the wide range of programs for which Python is used, it's difficult to give general advice for making code run faster. However, there are a few universal guidelines that may be of use.

File (and network) input/output is slow

Due to the physical layout of computer systems, it's generally many orders of magnitude quicker to read and write data to memory than to files (this is true in all languages, not just Python). For many programs, the slowest step is going to be reading in the data files and writing to the output files. The speed of reading/writing files is determined by the hardware, so there's not much we can do to speed it up.

What we **can** often do is minimise the amount of input/output in our program. At the simplest level, this means ensuring that we never read the same data from disk twice. Be especially careful about reading files inside loops. If you need to process data from the same file multiple times, don't read the file multiple times like this:

Chapter 5:Performance

```
for i in range(10):
    myfile = open("input.txt")
    for line in myfile:
        print(line[0:i])
    myfile.close()
```

Instead, use `readlines()` to make a list of lines in the file:

```
lines = open("input.txt").readlines()
for i in range(10):
    for line in lines:
        print(line[0:i])
```

Similarly, when writing output, it's often easy to leave in debugging and status messages:

```
for i in range(100000):
    print("processing number: " + str(i))
    # real processing code goes here
```

but remember that printing to a terminal also counts as input/output so can be very slow. A useful trick if you want to show progress is to only print a status message every thousand iterations[1]:

```
for i in range(10000):
    if i % 1000 == 0: # if i is a multiple of 1000
        print("processing number: " + str(i))
    # real processing code goes here
```

```
processing number: 0
processing number: 1000
processing number: 2000
processing number: 3000
processing number: 4000
...
```

---

1   See the description of progress bars in the chapter on building user interfaces for another approach.

Another strategy to minimise input/output is to carefully consider the format that you use to pass data between programs as part of a work flow. If you're going to run program A to create a data file, then run program B to analyse it, picking a compact data format will help to speed up both programs. Three options worth looking into are:

- using the `pickle` module[1] to directly write and read Python data structures to and from files
- using a lightweight format like json[2] to store data in
- compressing output/input files using the `gzip` module[3]

Network operations (i.e. fetching a web page or calling an API) are also slow – not only do you have the overhead of transferring data, you also have to wait for the response from the server. A fairly common pattern in bioinformatics work is to get a list of identifiers (e.g. of genes or proteins) then retrieve information about them in a loop:

```
my_ids = ['abc123', 'def456', ...]
for id in my_ids:
    data = urllib2.urlopen('http://example.org/protein/' + id)
    # do something with data
```

If the list of identifiers contains duplicates, then this wastes a lot of time downloading the same information repeatedly: it would be better to either avoid duplicates or cache the result (see the section below on duplicating data). For many online resources, the best way to speed up code is to make a local copy of the database, thus avoiding the need for network input entirely.

---

1 https://docs.python.org/2/library/pickle.html
2 https://docs.python.org/2/library/json.html
3 https://docs.python.org/2/library/gzip.html

Use existing modules and algorithms

It's an established principle of programming that the same basic problems occur again and again, even in wildly different fields. This turns out to be good news for programmers, since it means that when we encounter a problem there's often an existing solution that we can use.

For example, imagine we have a list of genes and a list of species. For each species, only some of the genes are available in public sequence databases. Our goal is to narrow down the list of genes and species so that all genes are available for all species, while keeping the lists as big as possible.

At first glance this sounds like a very biology specific problem, and we can start imagining ways that we might try to write a program to solve it – for example, repeatedly removing the species with the lowest number of genes available. However, this is actually an example of a well known problem called *biclustering* (which has nothing to do with biology).

Since this problem has already been studied, algorithms have already been designed to solve it[1]. These existing algorithms probably have better performance than anything we are likely to invent starting from scratch, so it makes sense to use them. If we are lucky, there may already be a Python module that implements the algorithm, thus freeing us from the obligation to write any code at all!

In general, mature Python modules are likely to be well optimized, so using them will not only allow us to develop our program faster but will make our programs run faster too. Mature modules have other advantages as well: they can sometimes take advantage of advanced techniques for improving performance that might be beyond our reach.

---

1   http://www.kemaleren.com/the-bimax-algorithm.html

Chapter 5:Performance

For example, network analysis is widely used in biology in fields ranging from gene expression to ecology. The `graph-tool` package[2] is designed to solve network analysis problems. Not only does it include many useful algorithms and data structures, it uses advanced Python features (notably the ability to write some of the code in a much faster language) to achieve performance far better than any code we are likely to write ourselves.

Don't calculate the same thing multiple times

A common error is to write code that repeatedly carries out the same calculation. We saw a good example of this kind of error in the chapter on automated testing when we wrote the following function to identify commonly occurring kmers in a DNA sequence:

```
def find_common_kmers(dna, k, threshold):
    result = set()
    for start in range(len(dna)):
        kmer = dna[start:start+k]
        if dna.count(kmer) >= threshold and kmer not in result:
            result.add(kmer)
    return result
```

Because this code calls `dna.count(kmer)` for every kmer start position in the DNA sequence, it will end up counting the same kmer multiple times. A quick fix is to use a separate set to remember which kmers we've already counted❶, and only count new kmers:

---

2   https://graph-tool.skewed.de/

```
def find_common_kmers_quick(dna, k, threshold):
    result = set()
    seen_kmers = set()❶
    for start in range(len(dna)):
        kmer = dna[start:start+k]
        if kmer not in seen_kmers:❷
            seen_kmers.add(kmer)
            if dna.count(kmer) >= threshold:
                result.add(kmer)
    return result
```

On my computer with a 10 kilobase DNA sequence and k=4, the first version of the function takes ~450 milliseconds while the second only takes ~14 milliseconds.

Often we need the same bit of information multiple times in a program. Here's a simple example: given a list of DNA sequences, we want to print out all the ones that contain one A, then all the ones that contain two A's, and so on up to ten A's:

```
for a_count in range(1,11):
    print('these sequences contain ' + str(a_count) + 'A bases')
    for dna in sequences:
        if dna.count('A') == a_count:
            print(dna)
```

This code is very inefficient, because for each DNA sequence it will end up calculating the number of A's ten times, getting the same answer in each case. Better to calculate the number of A's for each sequence and store them in a dict, then look up that value whenever it's needed:

Chapter 5:Performance

```
seq_count = {}
for dna in sequences:
    seq_count[dna] = dna.count('A')

for a_count in range(1,11):
    print('these sequences contain ' + str(a_count) + ' A bases')
    for dna in sequences:
        if seq_count[dna] == a_count:
            print(dna)
```

Sometimes duplicated effort can be a bit more subtle and harder to spot. Imagine we have a function that takes two DNA sequences and calculates some measure of similarity:

```
def calculate_similarity(sequence_one, sequence_two):
    # some complex calculations....
    return similarity
```

The details aren't important, but let's assume that this function is slow to run so we want to minimize the number of times it's called. If we want to identify similar pairs of sequences from a list, we might start of by writing two nested `for` loops like this:

```
sequences = ['ACTGCA', 'TCGCCA', ...]
for dna1 in sequences:
    for dna2 in sequences:
        if calculate_similarity(dna1, dna2) > 0.9:
            print(dna1 + ' is similar to ' + dna2)
```

This will work, but will call the `calculate_similarity()` function more than twice as many times as needed, because it will call both

```
calculate_similarity(sequences[0], sequences[1])
```

and

```
calculate_similarity(sequences[1], sequences[0])
```

and will also compare each sequence to itself.

We can avoid these unnecessary comparisons by rewriting the loops to only compare each sequence to those that come after it in the list:

```
for i in range(len(sequences)):
    for j in range(i+1, len(sequences)):
        dna1 = sequences[i]
        dna2 = sequences[j]
        if calculate_similarity(dna1, dna2) > 0.9:
            print(dna1 + ' is similar to ' + dna2)
```

Unsurprisingly, generating these kind of pairwise combinations is a common problem in programming, so we could also use the built in `itertools` module to do the work for us:

```
import itertools

# generate all possible combinations of two elements from sequences
for dna1, dna2 in itertools.combinations(sequences, 2):
    if calculate_similarity(dna1, dna2) > 0.9:
        print(dna1 + ' is similar to ' + dna2)
```

Avoid loops if possible

For very simple loops – i.e. when the body of the loop doesn't involve any slow code – the overhead of keeping track of Python's position in the loop can be significant. For example: imagine we have a big list of DNA sequences and we want to create a list of their lengths. The most obvious solution is probably a loop:

```
sequences = ['ACTGCA', 'TCGCCA', ...]
lengths = []
for s in sequences:
    lengths.append(len(s))
```

Chapter 5:Performance

However, if we profile this code, we'll see that only 60% of the time is spent calculating and appending the length. The remaining 40% of the time is spent iterating over the loop.

An alternative is to avoid an explicit loop by using map()[1]:

```
lengths = map(len, sequences)
```

This code is more concise and about twice as fast, because the bit of code responsible for iterating over the list is the built in map() function which is actually written in C rather than in Python. Another option which is equally fast is a list comprehension[2]:

```
lengths = [len(s) for s in sequences]
```

Things get slightly more complicated when we have a more complex loop body. Imagine we now want to take our list of DNA sequence lengths and divide each one by three to get a list of corresponding protein lengths. As before, let's start with a loop:

```
protein_lengths = []
for l in lengths:
    protein_lengths.append(l / 3)
```

Rewriting this to use map() is a bit more complicated than before: there's no built in divide_by_three() function, so we have to either write one:

```
def divide_by_three(x):
    return x / 3

protein_lengths = map(divide_by_three, lengths)
```

---

1   See the chapter on functional programming in *Advanced Python for Biologists* for a detailed description of map().
2   See the chapter on iterators, comprehensions and generators in *Advanced Python for Biologists* for a detailed explanation of list comprehensions.

or use a lambda expression:

```
protein_lengths = map(lambda x : x/3 , lengths)
```

but unlike the previous example, both of these are actually slower than the loop due to the extra time taken to look up the function call. The winner in this case is the comprehension:

```
protein_lengths = [x / 3 for x in  lengths]
```

because it allows us to express the transformation without defining a function or using a lambda expression – the comprehension is about twice as fast as the loop or the `map()`.

Avoid searching through lists

When working with lists of things – particularly complex data structures – it's easy to fall into situations where we iterate over the list in order to find a single element. Consider the situation where we have a list of DNA sequence records, each stored as a tuple[1]:

```
records = [
    ('actgctagt', 'ABC123', 1),
    ('ttaggttta', 'XYZ456', 1),
    ('cgcgatcgt', 'HIJ789', 5)
    ...
]
```

For each DNA sequence we are storing the sequence itself, an accession number, and a genetic code[2]. To find a specific record we might iterate over the list:

---

1 See the chapter on data structures in *Advanced Python for Biologists* for a description of this particular way of storing sequence records.
2 You can imagine this example with sequence record objects instead of tuples; the argument remains the same.

Chapter 5:Performance

```
# find the DNA sequence with accession number XYZ456
for record in records:
    if record[1] == 'XYZ456'
        seq = record[0]
        # do something with the sequence
```

However, this will be very slow if we need to look up many records, since we have to examine, on average, half of the elements in the list before we find the one we're looking for. A better solution might be to store the records as a dict where the key is the accession number and the value is a tuple containing the sequence and genetic code:

```
records = {
    'ABC123' : ('actgctagt', 1),
    'XYZ456' : ('ttaggttta', 1),
    'HIJ789' : ('cgcgatcgt', 5)
    ...
}
```

Now looking up the sequence for a given accession number is extremely fast:

```
# find the DNA sequence with accession number XYZ456
record = records['XYZ456']
seq = record[0]
# do something with the sequence
```

Take care with the order of complex conditions

When Python encounters a complex condition of the form `X and Y`, it carries out a subtle bit of optimization. It first checks condition `X`, and if `X` is false, then it doesn't have to check `Y`, because the entire complex condition will be false regardless of `Y`. This behaviour is called *short-circuiting*.

We can take advantage of this by putting the condition that's quickest to check first. Here's a bit of code that will generate a list of 1000 DNA sequences of 1Kb length for testing:

```
import random

# function to generate a random DNA sequence
def random_dna(l):
    return "".join([random.choice(['A','T','G','C']) for _ in range(l)])

# use a list comprehension to make a list of DNA sequences
dnas = [random_dna(1000) for i in range(1000)]
```

Imagine we want to make a new list consisting of just the sequences that have an AT content greater than 0.5 and that start with A. For any single sequence, we can test this in either order:

```
# check the AT content first
(dna.count('A') + dna.count('T')) / len(dna) > 0.5 and dna.startswith('A')

# check the starting base first
dna.startswith('A') and (dna.count('A') + dna.count('T')) / len(dna) > 0.5
```

and the result will be exactly the same. However, let's look at what happens when we test each sequence in a loop. Using the first version:

```
chosen = []

for dna in dnas:
    if (
        (dna.count('A') + dna.count('T')) / len(dna) > 0.5 and
        dna.startswith('A')
    ):
        chosen.append(dna)
```

Python has to calculate the AT content – a relatively slow step – for every single sequence. Using the second version:

Chapter 5:Performance

```
chosen = []

for dna in dnas:
    if (
        dna.startswith('A') and
        (dna.count('A') + dna.count('T')) / len(dna) > 0.5
    ):
        chosen.append(dna)
```

Python only has to calculate the AT content for sequences which start with A (which is quick to check). These two loops give exactly the same result, but thanks to short circuiting the second version is around four times faster on my computer. This is what we'd expect, as about a quarter of randomly generated sequences start with a given base.

This example works because one of the conditions – checking the AT content – is much **slower** than the other. We can also take advantage of short-circuiting where one condition is **less likely to be true** than the other. Let's take the same list of DNA sequences and extract just the ones that have more than 210 A's and fewer than 210 C's. Just as before, there are two different ways to express the complex condition: we can check the A count first:

```
chosen = []
for dna in dnas:
    if dna.count('A') > 210 and dna.count('C') < 210:
        chosen.append(dna)
```

or we can check the C count first:

```
chosen = []
for dna in dnas:
    if dna.count('C') < 210 and dna.count('A') > 210:
        chosen.append(dna)
```

The amount of work involved in testing these two conditions is about the same, so we might expect the order not to matter. However, when we test it, the second version is around twice as fast as the first.

The reason is that the condition `dna.count('A') > 210` is going to be true for nearly all the DNA sequences (remember they are 1000 bases long, so we expect each one to have 250 A's on average). When we test this condition first, the result is nearly always true, so we nearly always have to go on and test the other condition.

In contrast, the condition `dna.count('C') < 210` is nearly always going to be false, so when we test it first, we rarely have to proceed to counting the number of A's

This short-circuiting trick works for complex conditions using `or` as well, but remember that for `or` the first condition should be the one which is **most** likely to be true.

Further topics in performance

The techniques that we've discussed in this chapter – benchmarking, profiling, and incremental improvement – will probably be sufficient to tackle the majority of performance related issues you encounter in day to day programming. If you need even more speed, there are many other options to investigate; we don't have room to cover them in depth, but these suggestions may be useful starting points for your search.

Parallelization

If the problem you're trying to solve is amenable to **parallelization** (and many biological problems are) then the largest speed boost you can get is likely to come from writing parallel code. Many libraries exist to help you with this, but the best starting point is probably the `multiprocessing` module[1], which is part of the Python standard library. In particular, if you can write the core part of your program as a call to the `map()` function, you can probably turn it into a parallel version very easily.

Extending Python in other languages

Often, there's a small part of a program which takes up the vast majority of the execution time (which we can now easily identify using the profiling tools described earlier in this chapter). A powerful technique to speed up code is to rewrite this part of the program in a faster language[2] – typically C or C++. Obviously this approach is only useful if you can already program in C! Take a look at the official Python docs[3] or the `cffi` library[4].

Use a database

If your problem involves a very large amount of data, then storing it in flat files on disk and in memory in Python programs might not work well. Relational Database Management Systems (RDBMSs) are specialized pieces of software designed to do one thing extremely well: manage large volumes of data. For many data heavy problems, a good strategy is to use a database to handle storing, filtering, sorting and validating your data, then write a Python program which can talk to the database and extract the information needed for a particular analysis.

If you're already familiar with a particular RDBMS, take a look at the list of Python database interfaces[5] to find a module that will allow you to connect

---

1 https://docs.python.org/2/library/multiprocessing.html
2 A discussion of how to determine whether one language is faster than another is well beyond the scope of this book: suffice it to say that, for some specific problems, we can write a faster solution in another language than we can in Python.
3 https://docs.python.org/2/extending/extending.html
4 http://cffi.readthedocs.org/en/latest/index.html
5 https://wiki.python.org/moin/DatabaseInterfaces

to it from inside a Python program. If not, take a look at the `sqlite3` module, which is part of the Python standard library.

Try PyPy

When you run a Python program, what you're actually doing is giving your source code to a Python *interpreter* (a program whose job it is to run Python programs). The "standard" Python interpreter – and the one which you have probably always used – is called **CPython** because it's written in C. However, there are several different Python interpreters. Of particular relevance to this chapter is one called **PyPy**[1], which aims to be both faster and more memory efficient than CPython. Most Python programs can be run on PyPy without any modification, so it's a quick way to get a possible improvement in performance.

Take advantage of existing packages

Many well written Python packages and modules contain optimizations to make sure that code runs quickly. Of particular interest to us is the scientific Python stack[2], an extremely high quality collection of packages that work together for scientific Python programming. If you are writing Python programs that involve numerical computation on lists of things, take a look at the `NumPy`[3] package which is highly optimized for these types of tasks. If you have code that involves a lot of maths, take a look at the `Numba` module, which may require you to tweak your code a bit but can deliver impressive performance.

---

1   http://pypy.org/
2   http://www.scipy.org/index.html
3   http://www.numpy.org/

Recap

Measuring, describing and improving the performance of Python code is a complicated topic; it's no surprise that this is one of the longest chapters in this book. We started by covering the difference between **benchmarking** (measuring how long a piece of code takes to run) and **profiling** (finding out which bits of code take the most time to run). In general, benchmarking is most useful when experimenting with different ways of writing a new piece of code, whereas profiling is most useful when taking an existing piece of code and making it run faster.

As we've seen, there are a few common pitfalls when optimizing Python code. Trying to optimize code without profiling it (or trying to optimize after profiling it with unrealistic data) can easily lead to you wasting time working on the wrong thing. Also, don't fall into the trap of spending more time optimizing code than you will save when running it!

For any given optimization problem, there are generally a series of escalating steps that you can go through to speed your code up. Simple things like changing the order of conditions will often buy you a certain amount of speed up, but after these small changes have been made the only way to speed your code up further is with more drastic changes. Part of the skill of optimization is picking the right trade off between the speed you need and the amount of coding effort you have to expend to get it.

6: Building user interfaces

Why do we need a user interface?

As we discussed in the chapter on packaging and distributing Python code, most pieces of software (at least for scientific work) begin life as a few lines of code that attempt to solve an immediate problem. These early programs tend to have a few defining features:

- They are structurally simple; they don't make use of custom classes and are not split over multiple modules
- They just do a single job, and don't have many options and parameters
- The person who uses the program is the same person who wrote it

As projects progress, and software tools become larger, they change in nature:

- They become more structurally complex, maybe involving code spread over multiple modules, divided into client and library code, and involving custom classes, exception types, etc.
- They start to become more flexible, with different options, parameters, input and output file formats, etc.
- They start to be used by more than one person and may be distributed to people who work in different places, and who are not themselves programmers

At some point along this line, it becomes necessary to think about providing a user interface for the program. At the start of their life, when programs are small, structurally simple, and used only by the author,

Chapter 6: Building user interfaces

there's no need for an interface. If we've written a small program and we need to change its behaviour, we can just go in and edit the code, changing the value of a variable, or changing the name of an input file.

But when the program becomes more complex and widely used, this is no longer satisfactory. In a larger program, it can be hard to figure out which bits of the code need to be changed, and it's easy to make mistakes when code is spread over multiple modules. It's also inefficient to have to switch to editing the code whenever we want to make a small change to a parameter. And if the person using the code is not a programmer, it's obviously a bad idea to ask them to go and start fiddling with the code just to change the name of the output file.

Fortunately for us, Python has a collection of useful libraries which make it easy for us to build user interfaces for our programs. Normally when we talk about user interfaces we think of a point-and-click, graphical interface, but for the purposes of this chapter, a user interface is anything that allows the user to interact with your program – including command line, graphical, and web interfaces.

As we'll see in this chapter, there's a whole spectrum of complexity of user interfaces, from a single line of code that asks the user for a parameter to a graphical interface with windows, buttons and visualization tools. In this chapter we'll look at examples of various different types of interface, and discuss when each should be used and some best practices for doing so.

A quick note: in the examples that follow, I'll be talking about "the user" on the assumption that the person using the program is not the person who wrote the program. However, everything I'm going to say applies equally for programs where the author is also the main user – anything which you do to make life easier for your hypothetical users also makes life easier for you when you are using your own software!

A simple program

Let's begin with an example of the type of early program we just described. Here's a piece of code that reads a DNA sequence from a file, counts the number of unique 4mers (overlapping short 4-base sequences), and prints out just the 4mers that make up more than one percent of the total number:

```
from __future__ import division
import collections

dna = open("dna.txt").read().rstrip("\n")
all_fourmers = []

for start in range(len(dna) - 3):❶
    fourmer = dna[start:start+4]❷
    all_fourmers.append(fourmer)

fourmer_counts = collections.Counter(all_fourmers)❸
total_count = len(all_fourmers)

for fourmer, count in fourmer_counts.items():❹
    fraction = count / total_count
    if fraction > 0.01:
        print(fourmer, count, fraction)
```

find_4mers.py

Hopefully the logic of the program is fairly easy to follow. After opening and reading the input file, we use a `range()` ❶ to iterate over the list of 4mer start positions (0,1,2, etc. up to four bases before the end of the DNA string). For each start position, we add four to get the stop position, then extract the substring from the DNA between those two positions ❷ and append it to a list of 4mers. We use a `collections.Counter`[1] to count

---

[1] If you've never encountered `collections.Counter` before, it's a special type of dict that takes an iterable – in this case, our list of 4mers – and creates a dict where the keys are the unique elements and the counts are the number of times each unique element occurs.

Chapter 6: Building user interfaces

the number of times each 4mer occurs in the list❸, then iterate over the 4mers and their counts❹ in order to figure out which ones to print.

We can consider this the first stage in the evolution of this program – it does a single job, is pretty unstructured, and is unlikely to be useful to anyone other than the person who wrote it. When we run it on a test input (the file *dna.txt* actually contains the sequence for *C. elegans* chromosome one) we get the expected output:

```
('AAAT', 271034, 0.017728834018816763)
('AAAA', 447410, 0.029265913606259023)
('GAAA', 185947, 0.012163136356681896)
('AATT', 250026, 0.016354661977422316)
('TTTC', 187271, 0.012249741639564904)
('TTTT', 452649, 0.029608606262621625)
('ATTT', 273619, 0.017897923638342878)
```

There are seven 4mers that each make up more than one percent of the total number[1].

What happens if we want to do the same but for 6mers rather than 4mers? There are two numbers we have to change: the number that we subtract from the length of the sequence to get the end of the range of start positions❶, and the number that we add to each start position to get the stop position for a given 6mer❷:

```
...
for start in range(len(dna) - 3):❶
    fourmer = dna[start:start+4]❷
    all_fourmers.append(fourmer)
...
```

To make life easier, let's make a second version of our program that can count short sequences of any length (which we'll refer to from now on as

---
[1] Incidentally, glancing at the composition of these 4mers tells us something about the AT-richness of the *C. elegans* genome.

kmers). We'll create variables at the start of the program to hold the kmer length, the reporting threshold, and the input file name❶.

```
from __future__ import division
import collections

input_filename = "dna.txt" ❶
kmer_length = 4
threshold = 0.01

dna = open(input_filename).read().rstrip("\n")
all_kmers = []
for start in range(len(dna) - kmer_length + 1):
    kmer = dna[start:start+kmer_length]
    all_kmers.append(kmer)

kmer_counts = collections.Counter(all_kmers)
total_count = len(all_kmers)

for kmer, count in kmer_counts.items():
    fraction = count / total_count
    if fraction > threshold:
        print(kmer, count, fraction)
```

find_kmers.py

Running this program gives us exactly the same output as before, but now if we want to change the name of the input file, the length of the kmers, or the threshold for printing a kmer it's obvious what bit of the code we need to edit. For example, to count the number of 6mers that make up more than half a percent of the total we just change the first few lines:

```
input_filename = "dna.txt"
kmer_length = 6
threshold = 0.005

...
```

Chapter 6:Building user interfaces

Although this makes running the program easier for us, the programmer, we can't really describe it as a user interface. Changing the behaviour of the program still requires editing the code.

A simple interactive interface

The simplest interface we can add to our program is one which asks the user for the information it requires. To do this, we use the `raw_input()` function (in Python 3, this function is simply called `input()`) to provide a prompt and store what the user types.

Our first attempt will probably look something like this:

```
input_filename = raw_input("Enter the input file name:\n")
kmer_length = raw_input("Enter the kmer length:\n")
threshold = raw_input("Enter the threshold:\n")

...
```

but this will quickly fail with a `TypeError` – we must remember that whenever we use `raw_input()` the returned value is a string, so if we want an integer (for the kmer length) or a float (for the threshold) we have to convert them. This works fine:

```
input_filename = raw_input("Enter the input file name:\n")
kmer_length = int(raw_input("Enter the kmer length:\n"))
threshold = float(raw_input("Enter the threshold:\n"))

...
```

find_kmers_raw_input.txt

and gives the expected output.

Giving feedback to the user

Interactive inputs like this have a lot to recommend them at first: they're very easy to write, and because each input comes with a helpful prompt, they're often easy for non-programmers to use. We have to be careful about when to ask for interactive input – consider this version of the program which doesn't ask for the threshold until it's actually needed ❶:

```
input_filename = raw_input("Enter the input file name:\n")
kmer_length = int(raw_input("Enter the kmer length:\n"))

dna = open(input_filename).read().rstrip("\n")
all_kmers = []
for start in range(len(dna) - kmer_length + 1):
    kmer = dna[start:start+kmer_length]
    all_kmers.append(kmer)

kmer_counts = collections.Counter(all_kmers)
total_count = len(all_kmers)

threshold = float(raw_input("Enter the threshold:\n"))  ❶
for kmer, count in kmer_counts.items():
    fraction = count / total_count
    if fraction > threshold:
        print(kmer, count, fraction)
```

find_kmers_late_input.py

If you try running this example, you'll see why this is a bad design: there's a long pause between when it asks for the kmer length and when it asks for the threshold. This is because the process of splitting up the sequence into kmers and counting them is fairly time consuming. In this version of the code, the user has to sit in front of the keyboard waiting to enter the threshold (or wondering why they haven't been asked for it), rather than giving all the information at the start of the program then leaving to get a cup of coffee while it runs!

Chapter 6:Building user interfaces

The relatively long running time of this program[1] leads us to another point about user interfaces: it's a good idea to provide some reassurance to the user that your program is actually running. This can be as simple as a status message letting them know that something is happening:

```
input_filename = raw_input("Enter the input file name:\n")
kmer_length = int(raw_input("Enter the kmer length:\n"))
threshold = float(raw_input("Enter the threshold:\n"))

print("counting kmers, this may take a while...")
...
```

For a long running program (and we tend to encounter plenty of those in bioinformatics) it's often very useful to know how long we have to wait. The `tqdm` module allows us to add an incredibly useful progress bar to our program with very few additions to the code. We'll need to install the `tqdm` module:

`$ pip install tqdm`

then wrap the thing we want to iterate over – in this case, our `range()` – in a call to the `tqdm()` function:

```
from tqdm import tqdm

...
for start in tqdm(range(len(dna) - kmer_length + 1)):
    kmer = dna[start:start+kmer_length]
    all_kmers.append(kmer)
...
```

find_kmers_progress.py

With this single extra bit of code, we get a progress bar which visually displays the progress of our program, along with useful bits of information

---

1 A few seconds on my desktop computer using the test input; it will be much longer for a bigger input e.g. a complete genome.

Chapter 6:Building user interfaces

like the total number of iterations, the estimated time until completion, and the number of iterations per second. While the program is running, it looks like this[1]:

45%|███████| | 6287751/15287751 [00:03<00:05, 2880251.63it/s]

which tells the user that

- the program is 45% done
- 6287751 out of a total of 15287751 kmers have been counted
- three seconds have elapsed and five seconds are remaining
- it's processing 2880251 kmers per second.

Quite a lot of information for such a small amount of code!

If you try running this example on a bigger input (or a slow computer) you'll notice that the progress bar is actually a bit optimistic – there's another pause between when the progress bar finishes and when the output is displayed. That's because the step where we build the `Counter` object:

```
kmer_counts = collections.Counter(all_kmers)
```

takes quite a bit of time, but is outside the progress bar loop. We could fix this by initializing an empty `Counter` object and updating it inside the loop:

---

[1] Obviously a static image can't really capture what's going on here, so I strongly encourage you to try running this example yourself.

Chapter 6:Building user interfaces

```
...
kmer_counts = collections.Counter()

for start in tqdm(range(len(dna) - kmer_length + 1), unit="kmer"):
    kmer = dna[start:start+kmer_length]
    kmer_counts.update([kmer])
...
```

This makes the progress bar more accurate as more of the computational work is now taking place inside the loop.

A simple command line interface

Although the interactive interface described above has a lot to recommend it, it has some serious limitations for large scale use. Because it's interactive, it relies on the user typing in the necessary information at the right time, so there's no way to automate it. In bioinformatics work we often want to run a program in an automated way – for example, to run the same program on multiple datasets, or to run a program repeatedly with different parameters, or to run a program as part of an automated pipeline.

The easiest way to make our program amenable to automation is to switch from interactive input to command line input[1]. In other words, instead of running our program like this:

```
$ python count_kmers.py
```

and then providing interactive input, we'd like to be able to run it like this:

```
$ python count_kmers.py dna.txt 4 0.01
```

and supply all the necessary information (the input file name, the kmer length, and the threshold) on the command line.

---

[1] If you don't actually use the command line for your own work, then some of this section may not make much sense. Just remember that even if you don't use the command line, some of the users of your program may do.

Doing this is quite straightforward. When we run a Python program with command line arguments, the arguments are stored as strings in a list variable argv in the sys module. So to access them, we simply import the sys module, then assign each element of the sys.argv list to the appropriate variable for our program:

```
import sys

input_filename = sys.argv[1]
kmer_length = int(sys.argv[2])
threshold = float(sys.argv[3])

print("counting kmers, this may take a while...")
...
```

find_kmers_argv.py

There are two important things to note here. Firstly, the first element of sys.argv (i.e. sys.argv[0]) holds the name of the Python program (in our case, find_kmers_argv.py), so the command line arguments that we want start at the second element (i.e. sys.argv[1]). Secondly, just like with interactive input, command line options are always returned as strings, so we have to explicitly turn the kmer length and the threshold into an integer and a float respectively.

This command line approach has clear advantages over the interactive one: if you're familiar with the command line, you can probably already imagine how you might use the program in a shell script or an alias[1]. The command line can also act as a record of what parameters were used to run a program – if you copy and paste the command line into a text document, you can refer back to it to see exactly what kmer length and threshold you used. And replicating the analysis can be done simply by copying and pasting the command line back into your terminal program.

---

1   If you're not familiar with the command line, then don't worry – just trust me that this version is much more flexible than the interactive one.

Chapter 6:Building user interfaces

However, the command line interface above has drawbacks too – most significantly, it doesn't offer any clue to the user about how to supply the arguments. With the interactive version, simply running the program was enough to start displaying helpful prompts, but if we run this version without any command line arguments we just get a very unhelpful error message:

```
$ python find_kmers_argv.py
Traceback (most recent call last):
  File "find_kmers_argv.py", line 5, in <module>
    input_filename = sys.argv[1]
IndexError: list index out of range
```

The minimum we can do to help the user is to print some instructions if the program is run without command line arguments. The `sys.exit()` function will print the argument and terminate the program, which allows us to write something like this:

```
if len(sys.argv) != 4:
    sys.exit("Usage: python find_kmers_usage.py input_filename kmer_length threshold")

# if we get to here, then the input is valid
input_filename = sys.argv[1]
kmer_length = int(sys.argv[2])
threshold = float(sys.argv[3])

...
```

find_kmers_usage.py

Now running the program without any command line arguments results in a slightly better user experience:

```
$ python count_kmers.py
Usage: python count_kmers.py input_filename kmer_length threshold
```

Of course, you can also tell the novice user where to get help:

```
if len(sys.argv) != 4:
    sys.exit("Ask Dave for help with this program")
```

or direct them to documentation:

```
if len(sys.argv) != 4:
    sys.exit("See http://www.example.com/count_kmers for help")
```

Input validation

As soon as we allow our program to accept input from the user – whether interactive or command line – we have to think about a whole new class of problems that might arise: invalid input. Even for our very simple program we can easily come up with a list of things that might go wrong:

- the file name might not exist
- the kmer length might not be an integer
- the user might give the threshold as a percentage rather than a proportion

Here we have a mixture of things that will cause the program to exit with an error (e.g. if the file doesn't exist) or produce meaningless output (e.g. if the threshold is given as a percentage).

We could think about adding some input validation code to our program to cope with these problems. For example, we might check that the file exists before we start to read it:

Chapter 6:Building user interfaces

```
import sys
import os

input_filename = sys.argv[1]

if not os.path.exists(input_filename):
    sys.exit("Incorrect filename!")
```
...

This take care of the situation where the specified input file doesn't exist, but there are other problems that might arise. For example, if the file exists but the user doesn't have the right permissions to read it, then our check will pass and the user will see an `IOError` traceback.

For file input, a good approach to validation is to take advantage of Python's built in exception system[1]. We can wrap the file input code in a `try` block, and handle any problems by printing our own error message:

```
input_filename = sys.argv[1]
try:
    dna = open(input_filename).read().rstrip("\n")
except IOError as ex:
    sys.exit("Sorry, couldn't open the file: " + ex.strerror)
```

find_kmers_try.py

Notice how we make sure to only catch `IOErrors` (so that we are only dealing with problems concerning the input file) and how we use `ex.strerror` to include the error message from the exception as part of the output. Now when there is a problem with the input file, the user will see our message along with a hint about the cause of the problem. If the file is missing:

---

[1] See the chapter on exception handling in *Advanced Python for Biologists* for a detailed look at how exceptions work.

Chapter 6: Building user interfaces

```
$ python find_kmers_try.py missing.txt 4 0.01
Sorry, couldn't open the file: No such file or directory
```

if the user doesn't have the right permissions:

```
$ python find_kmers_try.py forbidden.txt 4 0.01
Sorry, couldn't open the file:  Permission denied
```

and if the user accidentally gives the name of a directory rather than a file:

```
$ python find_kmers_try.py my_folder 4 0.01
Sorry, couldn't open the file:  Is a directory
```

Of course, even with these safeguards in place the user can still break the program by, for instance, giving the name of a valid input file that doesn't contain data in the expected format.

Note that this approach is equally applicable to interactive input; we could just as easily write this:

```
input_filename = raw_input("Enter the input file name:\n")
try:
    dna = open(input_filename).read().rstrip("\n")
except IOError as ex:
    print("Sorry, couldn't open the file: " + ex.strerror)
```

How about the other problems we listed? Exceptions will allow us to check for a valid integer for the kmer length as well, this time by checking for an `ValueError`:

```
try:
    kmer_length = int(sys.argv[2])
except ValueError as ex:
    sys.exit("Invalid input for the kmer length")
```

This catches completely invalid kmer lengths:

```
$ python find_kmers_try_value.py dna.txt four 0.01
Invalid input for the kmer length
```

Chapter 6:Building user interfaces

but not cases where the user supplies a floating point number rather than an integer:

```
$ python count_kmers.py dna.txt 4.5 0.01
```

because Python will happily convert a floating point number to an integer by truncating it (i.e. removing the part after the decimal point). At this point we have to decide what we want our program to do if the user enters a floating point number for the kmer length. We could just allow the program to proceed with an error message, in which case we first convert the input to a float, print a warning if it's not an integer (using the `is_integer()` method of `float` objects), then convert it to an integer and proceed:

```
kmer_length = float(sys.argv[2])
    if not kmer_length.is_integer():
        print("Warning, the kmer length will be rounded down")
        print("Using kmer length of " + str(int(kmer_length)))
    kmer_length = int(kmer_length)
```

Alternatively, if we want this to be a fatal error, we can exit as before:

```
kmer_length = float(sys.argv[2])
    if not kmer_length.is_integer():
        sys.exit("Kmer length must be an integer")
    kmer_length = int(kmer_length)
```

While we're checking the kmer length, we might as well also make sure that it's positive:

```
kmer_length = float(sys.argv[2])
    if kmer_length < 1 or not kmer_length.is_integer():
        sys.exit("Kmer length must be a positive integer")
    kmer_length = int(kmer_length)
```

Finally, how about checking the value for the threshold? In this case we know that it should be a floating point number between zero and one, so the condition is quite straightforward:

```
threshold = float(sys.argv[3])
    if not 0 < threshold < 1:
        sys.exit("Threshold must be between 0 and 1")
```

When we look at the complete program after adding all these validation checks, we might be surprised to see that they now make up a majority of the code:

Chapter 6:Building user interfaces

```
if len(sys.argv) != 4:
    sys.exit("Usage: python count_kmers.py input_filename kmer_length threshold")

input_filename = sys.argv[1]
try:
    dna = open(input_filename).read().rstrip("\n")
except IOError as ex:
    sys.exit("Sorry, couldn't open the file: " + ex.strerror)

try:
    kmer_length = float(sys.argv[2])
    if not kmer_length.is_integer():
        sys.exit("Kmer length must be an integer")
    kmer_length = int(kmer_length)
except ValueError as ex:
    sys.exit("Invalid input for the kmer length" )

try:
    threshold = float(sys.argv[3])
    if not 0 < threshold < 1:
        sys.exit("Threshold must be between 0 and 1")
except ValueError as ex:
    sys.exit("Invalid input for the threshold" )

kmer_counts = collections.Counter()
for start in tqdm(range(len(dna) - kmer_length + 1)):
    kmer = dna[start:start+kmer_length]
    kmer_counts.update([kmer])

total_count = sum(kmer_counts.values())

for kmer, count in kmer_counts.items():
    fraction = count / total_count
    if fraction > threshold:
        print(kmer, count, fraction)
```

find_kmers_validation.py

Even this generous amount of validation code doesn't completely protect against user error – apart from the possibility of an incorrectly formatted file, there's still the scope for meaningless input values (e.g. a kmer length greater than the length of the sequence). For real world programs, we have to strike a sensible balance between preventing common errors, and trying to think of every possible thing that might go wrong.

Because input validation is a common problem, several of the modules that we'll look at later in the chapter include features which handle it. So for many programs we'll let a module handle the generic validation (checking for valid files, integers versus floats, etc.) and just write the checks that are specific to our program.

Command line interfaces with argparse

The approach to writing command line interfaces that we saw above – where we rely on the order of the command line arguments – works well for simple programs. Specifically, it works well for programs that always take exactly the same number of arguments (file name, kmer length and threshold for our example) and where each argument is always a single value.

However, there are many types of programs that require a more sophisticated interface. As soon as we need to allow for optional arguments, arguments with multiple values, default values for arguments, or true/false arguments, simply using `sys.argv` isn't enough – it's time to switch to a more structured approach.

If you're familiar with using programs from the command line (probably on a Linux or OSX machine) then you'll be aware of various conventions:

- running a program without any arguments will display usage instructions
- command line arguments generally start with a hyphen and a letter
- the `-h` argument normally displays the help text

Chapter 6: Building user interfaces

- some arguments have both short and long forms (e.g. `-h` and `-help`)

When writing our own programs it's a good idea to follow these conventions, as it makes it easier for users to figure out how to use them. Fortunately, Python's `argparse` module – part of the standard library – makes this easy.

Positional arguments

Let's start off by using `argparse` to reproduce the very simple interface we already had. To get started with `argparse` we import the module and create an `ArgumentParser` object:

```
import argparse
parser = argparse.ArgumentParser()
```

We then tell our `ArgumentParser` object what arguments to expect by calling the `add_argument()` method, then tell it to go ahead and parse the command line arguments by calling the `parse_args()` method. For now, we'll just add the file name argument by calling `add_argument()` with a single string which is the name of the argument:

```
parser.add_argument("input_filename")
args = parser.parse_args()
```

Notice how we store the result of `parser.parse_args()` in a new variable called `args`. Later in the program, when we want to use the input file name argument, we can get it from the `args` object:

```
dna = open(args.input_filename).read().rstrip("\n")
```

The command line argument has become a property of the `args` object which has the same name (`input_filename`) as the string which we passed to the `add_argument()` method. For clarity, I've removed all the validation code that we wrote earlier from these examples – we'll add it back in later.

Using `argparse` in this way allows us to supply the file name on the command line just like before:

```
$ python find_kmers_argparse.py dna.txt
```

but it also gives us a few other features. Running our program with no arguments will now produce a usage message:

```
$ python find_kmers_argparse.py
usage: find_kmers_argparse.py [-h] input_filename
```

and, as the usage message suggests, running it with the `-h` command line argument will display help:

```
$ python find_kmers_argparse.py -h
usage: find_kmers_argparse.py [-h] input_filename

positional arguments:
  input_filename

optional arguments:
  -h, --help      show this help message and exit
```

What's interesting about both these features is that we never explicitly added them or wrote any help text; `argparse` was able to figure out what the help text should be just from the information we gave it in `add_argument()`. We can make the help text even better by supplying a description of the `input_filename` argument, which we can do by calling `add_argument()` with the `help` keyword argument[1]:

---

1   One of the tricky things about discussing the `argparse` module is that we are using the word *argument* to refer both to arguments that are passed to the `add_argument()` method, and to arguments that are passed to our program on the command line. Hopefully this won't be too confusing!

Chapter 6:Building user interfaces

```
parser.add_argument("input_filename", help="the name of your DNA sequence
file")
```

find_kmers_help.py

Now running our program with the `-h` option will display that description as part of the help:

```
$ python find_kmers_help.py -h
usage: find_kmers_help.py [-h] input_filename

positional arguments:
  input_filename   the name of your DNA sequence file

...
```

Strings, integers and floats

Let's see what happens if we add the other two command line arguments. We'll make two more calls to `add_argument()` (with appropriate help text) and refer to them in the code using the `args` variable:❶

```
parser = argparse.ArgumentParser()

parser.add_argument("input_filename",
                    help="the name of your DNA sequence file")
parser.add_argument("kmer_length",
                    help="length of the kmers")
parser.add_argument("threshold",
                    help="minimum fraction of a kmer to be printed")
args = parser.parse_args()

dna = open(args.input_filename).read().rstrip("\n")  ❶

kmer_counts = collections.Counter()
for start in tqdm(range(len(dna) - args.kmer_length + 1)):  ❶
    kmer = dna[start:start+args.kmer_length]  ❶
    kmer_counts.update([kmer])

total_count = sum(all_kmers.values)

for kmer, count in kmer_counts.items():
    fraction = count / total_count
    if fraction > args.threshold:  ❶
        print(kmer, count, fraction)
```

The help message looks great:

```
$ python example.py -h
usage: example.py [-h] input_filename kmer_length threshold

positional arguments:
  input_filename  the name of your DNA sequence file
  kmer_length     length of the kmers
  threshold       minimum fraction of a kmer to be printed

optional arguments:
  -h, --help      show this help message and exit
```

But we run into problems when we actually try to run the program:

```
$ python example.py dna.txt 4 0.01
Traceback (most recent call last):
  ...
TypeError: unsupported operand type(s) for -: 'int' and 'str'
```

Chapter 6:Building user interfaces

It's the same error that we encountered at the start of the chapter: command line (or interactive) arguments are always strings. We could solve the problem like we did before by manually converting them:

```
real_kmer_length = int(args.kmer_length)
```

but a better option is to use the `type` argument to tell `argparse` that we're expecting an integer (to make it easier to read, the method call is split over multiple lines):

```
parser.add_argument(
    "kmer_length",
    help="length of the kmers",
    type=int)
```

find_kmers_types.py

This solves several problems. Firstly, it means that `argparse` will automatically convert the kmer length argument to an integer when parsing it, so we can happily use `args.kmer_length` later in our program without error. It also means that if the user supplies a command line argument that isn't an integer, `argparse` will spot the problem and exit with a reminder of the usage instructions and an error message:

```
$ python find_kmers_types.py dna.txt 4.5 0.01
usage: find_kmers_types.py [-h] input_filename kmer_length threshold
find_kmers_types.py: error: argument kmer_length: invalid int value: '4.5'
```

Let's do the same for the threshold argument, remembering that it's a floating point number rather than an integer:

```
parser.add_argument(
    "threshold",
    help="minimum fraction of a kmer to be printed",
    type=float)
```

find_kmers_types.py

Using `argparse` in this way allows us to get our command line arguments converted to the correct type, and adds input validation, without having to write any extra code.

Custom validation

Recall from our previous examples that we want to be quite strict about validation for the threshold: we want it to be a floating point number between zero and one. Passing `type=float` to the `add_argument()` method takes care of making sure that it is a floating point number, but doesn't address the restricted range. We could start writing separate validation code like we did before:

```
if not 0 < args.threshold < 1:
    ...
```

but that would mean that we no longer take advantage of `argparse`'s built in help system.

Coming up with a better solution requires us to figure out exactly how the `type` argument works. From the examples we've seen so far (`type=int` and `type=float`) it looks like we're giving the name of a Python class. However, what we're actually doing is giving the name of a Python function that will take the command line argument string and return the data in the correct type. For our examples, these are the `int()` and `float()` functions, both of which can take a string as input.

So to implement our custom validation, we just have to write a function that will take a command line argument string and return the correct type. To make our custom function work with `argparse`, we'll raise an `argparse.ArgumentTypeError` exception if the value is outside the allowed range:

Chapter 6:Building user interfaces

```
def check_float(threshold):
    result = float(threshold)
    if not 0 < result < 1:
        raise argparse.ArgumentTypeError("Threshold must be between 0 and 1")
    return result
```

find_kmers_check_float.py

Note that within this function, the call to `float()` will still raise the appropriate exception if a non-floating-point input string is entered.

To use this function for type conversion and validation, we pass its name to the `add_argument()` method:

```
parser.add_argument(
    "threshold",
    help="minimum fraction of a kmer to be printed",
    type=check_float)
```

find_kmers_check_float.py

Now we get the behaviour we want in all possible situations. If the threshold string is valid, it gets converted to a float and the program proceeds as normal. If it's a valid floating point number but not between 0 and 1 we get our custom error message along with a usage reminder:

```
$ python find_kmers_check_float.py dna.txt 4 1.5
usage: find_kmers_check_float.py [-h] input_filename kmer_length threshold

find_kmers_check_float.py: error: argument threshold: Threshold must be
between 0 and 1
```

And if it's not a valid floating point number we get a more generic error message:

```
$ python find_kmers_check_float.py dna.txt 4 banana
usage: find_kmers_check_float.py [-h] input_filename kmer_length threshold

find_kmers_check_float.py: error: argument threshold: invalid check_float
value: 'banana'
```

Of course, now we've added validation for the threshold, we should add the limits to the description:

```
parser.add_argument(
    "threshold",
    help="minimum fraction of a kmer to be printed (between 0 and 1)",
    type=check_float)
```

so that it's present in the help text:

```
$ python find_kmers_check_float.py -h
...
positional arguments:
 threshold      minimum fraction of a kmer to be printed (between 0 and 1)
...
```

We can add a similar custom validation function for the kmer length:

```
def check_kmer_length(kmer_length):
  result = int(kmer_length)
  if result < 1:
    raise argparse.ArgumentTypeError("Kmer length must be greater than 0")
  return result

...

parser.add_argument(
    "kmer_length",
    help="length of the kmers (greater than 0)",
    type=check_kmer_length)
```

find_kmers_check_float.py

Short and long arguments

If we take a close look at the help message for our program so far, we'll see that the `-h` option can actually take two forms: a short one (`-h`) and a long one (`--help`):

Chapter 6:Building user interfaces

```
$ python find_kmers_check_float.py -h
...

optional arguments:
 -h, --help      show this help message and exit
```

This is one of the conventions we mentioned earlier and, like most such conventions, it arose because it's useful. By having both short and long versions of options, the user of a program can construct a command line that's either short or explicit.

To add command line options like this to our program, we switch from using a simple argument name (like `kmer_length`) to a short and long argument form:

```
parser.add_argument(
    "-k",
    "--kmer_length",
    help="length of the kmers (greater than 0)",
    type=check_kmer_length)
```

find_kmers_optional.py

Our `add_argument()` method call now has four arguments: the short form, the long form, the description, and the name of the custom validation function. Let's see how this changes things by displaying the help text:

```
$ python find_kmers_optional.py -h
usage: count_kmers.py [-h] [-k KMER_LENGTH] input_filename threshold  ❶

positional arguments:
  input_filename        the name of your DNA sequence file
  threshold             minimum fraction of a kmer to be printed
                        (between 0 and 1)

optional arguments:  ❷
  -h, --help            show this help message and exit
  -k KMER_LENGTH, --kmer_length KMER_LENGTH  ❸❹
                        length of the kmers (greater than 0)
```

225

Four interesting things have happened. Firstly, the usage message has changed to show that the kmer length is now given by the `-k` flag❶: we now have to run our program like this:

```
$ python find_kmers_optional.py -k 4 dna.txt 0.01
```

Secondly, the kmer length has been moved from the *positional arguments* section to the *optional arguments* section❷. Thirdly, the help message now shows both short and long options for kmer length❸ – in other words, it informs us that we could also run our program like this:

```
$ python find_kmers_optional.py --kmer_length 4 dna.txt 0.01
```

Fourthly, the help message uses the name of the long option in capital letters (`KMER_LENGTH`) as a place holder when illustrating how to use the program❹.

If you try running this version of the program with the two command line examples above you'll see that the interface works just as described in the help. However, you might be a bit disturbed to see that the help message classifies the kmer length as an optional argument. This doesn't make much sense: there's no way that the program can run without a valid kmer length and if we try it, we'll quickly see that it causes an error:

```
$ python find_kmers_optional.py dna.txt 0.01
Traceback (most recent call last):
  ...
TypeError: unsupported operand type(s) for -: 'int' and 'NoneType'
```

The reason we're encountering this problem is that `argparse` is assuming that any argument whose name starts with a hyphen is optional. To fix this, we can add `required=True` to the `add_argument()` method call:

Chapter 6:Building user interfaces

```
parser.add_argument(
    "-k",
    "--kmer_length",
    help="length of the kmers (greater than 0)",
    type=check_kmer_length,
    required=True
    )
```

find_kmers_required.py

Now running the program without a kmer length produces a much more helpful error message:

```
$ python find_kmers_required.py dna.txt 0.01
usage: find_kmers_required.py y [-h] -k KMER_LENGTH input_filename
threshold
find_kmers_required.py: error: argument -k/--kmer_length is required
```

If we do the same for the threshold, we end up with code that looks like this:

```
...
parser.add_argument(
    "-k",
    "--kmer_length",
    help="length of the kmers (greater than 0)",
    type=check_kmer_length,
    required=True
    )

parser.add_argument(
    "-t",
    "--threshold",
    help="minimum fraction of a kmer to be printed (between 0 and 1)",
    type=check_float,
    required=True)
...
```

find_kmers_required.py

and a help message that looks like this:

```
usage: find_kmers_required.py [-h] -k KMER_LENGTH -t THRESHOLD
input_filename

positional arguments:
  input_filename         the name of your DNA sequence file

optional arguments:
  -h, --help             show this help message and exit
  -k KMER_LENGTH, --kmer_length KMER_LENGTH
                         length of the kmers (greater than 0)
  -t THRESHOLD, --threshold THRESHOLD
                         minimum fraction of a kmer to be printed
                         (between 0 and 1)
```

Using argument flags like this means that they can be supplied in any order – the following two command lines do exactly the same thing:

```
$ python find_kmers_required.py -k 4 -t 0.01 dna.txt
$ python find_kmers_required.py -t 0.01 -k 4 dna.txt
```

There's an obvious parallel here with keyword versus positional arguments in Python functions. Also important to notice in these examples is that the name of the input file is always last, and does not have a flag. There's no requirement for this to be the case – we could easily add a flag for the file name:

```
parser.add_argument(
    "-i",
    "--input_filename",
    help="the name of your DNA sequence file",
    required=True)
```

but it's a convention that input file names behave this way, so it's a good idea to stick to it.

Default argument values

At this point it makes sense to stop and consider whether the kmer length and threshold actually need to be required values. If, instead, we would

Chapter 6:Building user interfaces

rather pick a sensible default value then we just use `default` in the `add_argument()` method call rather than `required`:

```
...
parser.add_argument(
    "-k",
    "--kmer_length",
    help="length of the kmers (default: 4)",
    type=check_kmer_length,
    default=4
    )
parser.add_argument(
    "-t",
    "--threshold",
    help="minimum fraction of a kmer to be printed (default: 0.01)",
    type=check_float,
    default=0.01)
...
```

Notice how in this example we've also added the default value to the description so that it shows up when the help message is displayed. Using defaults where possible is generally a good design decision: it makes it easier for a user to get started with a program and means that they can override individual parameters when they want.

Boolean arguments

All the command line arguments that we've been looking at so far involve storing a value – the name of a file, the kmer length, or the threshold. However, some situations don't require a value. Imagine we wanted to make the progress bar optional. This might make sense if our program were being run as part of an automated pipeline: there's no point displaying the progress bar if there isn't a human there to see it!

Here's one way to do it: we could add a command line argument for the progress bar and get the user to supply the value T (for true) or F (for false):

```
parser.add_argument(
    "-p",
    "--progress",
    help="show progress bar (T or F)",
    default = "F"
)
```

Then later in the program we can use the value of that option to decide whether or not to use the `tqdm()` function:

```
if args.progress == "T":
    # if we want a progress bar, wrap the range in the tqdm function
    iterable = tqdm(range(len(dna) - args.kmer_length + 1))
else:
    # if not, just iterate over the range itself
    iterable = range(len(dna) - args.kmer_length + 1)

for start in iterable:
    kmer = dna[start:start+args.kmer_length]
    kmer_counts.update([kmer])
```

This works, but using T and F to represent the user's choice is inelegant. It's easy for the user to make mistakes like this:

```
$ python example.py -p True dna.txt
```

At a glance, it looks like this command line has set the -p flag to true and so the progress bar should be displayed, but because the string `"True"` doesn't equal the string `"T"`, it won't behave as expected. We could get round this by writing a custom validation function to only allow the values `"T"` and `"F"`, but that seems like too much code for a simple job.

Here's a better solution: if we tell `argparse` that the -p flag is a true/false option, then the user can simply add -p to the command line with no value

Chapter 6:Building user interfaces

and get the desired behaviour. To do this, we set the `action` argument to `"store_true"`:

```
parser.add_argument(
    "-p",
    "--progress",
    help="show progress bar (T or F)",
    action="store_true"
)
```

find_kmers_boolean.py

This changes the `-p`/`--progress` flag to a boolean value, so in the code we can just check it directly:

```
if args.progress:
    iterable = tqdm(range(len(dna) - args.kmer_length + 1))
else:
    iterable = range(len(dna) - args.kmer_length + 1)
...
```

When we want to show the progress bar on the command line, we simply add the -p flag without any accompanying value:

```
$ python find_kmers_boolean.py -p dna.txt
45%|████     | 6287751/15287751 [00:03<00:05, 2880251.63it/s]
```

This is reflected in the help text – notice how there's no place holder value for the -p flag either in the usage line or in the detailed list of arguments:

```
$ python find_kmers_boolean.py -h
usage: find_kmers_boolean.py [-h] [-k KMER_LENGTH] [-t THRESHOLD] [-p]
input_filename

optional arguments:
  -h, --help            show this help message and exit
  -k KMER_LENGTH, --kmer_length KMER_LENGTH
                        length of the kmers (greater than 0)
  -t THRESHOLD, --threshold THRESHOLD
                        minimum fraction of a kmer to be printed
                        (between 0 and 1)
  -p, --progress        show progress bar
```

Multiple values for options

An obvious extension for our program would be to analyse multiple kmer lengths in one run. We could do this quite easily in the code with a `for` loop:

```
k_values = [4,6,8]
for kmer_length in k_values:
    ..
```

but how might we implement an interface for it? One idea would be to have the user supply a minimum and maximum kmer length and then analyse all possible values:

Chapter 6:Building user interfaces

```
...
parser.add_argument(
    "-kmin",
    "--kmer_length_minimum",
    help="smallest kmer length to be analysed",
    type=int,
    default=4)

parser.add_argument(
    "-kmax",
    "--kmer_length_maximum",
    help="largest kmer length to be analysed",
    type=int,
    default=8)

...

for kmer_length in range(args.kmer_length_minimum,
args.kmer_length_maximum):
    print("Counting kmers of length " + str(kmer_length))

    ...
```

which works fine:

```
$ python example.py -p dna.txt
Counting kmers of length 4
...
Counting kmers of length 5
...
```

but is a bit inflexible. A better option would be to allow the user to specify a list of kmer lengths on the command line. To do this, we use the `nargs` keyword argument to `add_argument()`. The `nargs` argument can take various values[1], but for our purposes we want `'*'`, which will gather all the arguments under that option into a list:

---

1   See https://docs.python.org/2.7/library/argparse.html#nargs for details.

```
parser.add_argument(
    "-k",
    "--kmer_length",
    help="length of the kmers (greater than 0)",
    type=check_kmer_length,
    nargs = '*',
    default=[4,6,8]
    )
```

find_kmers_multiple.py

Note that we can still specify a default value as a list. Later in the code, we can refer to the list of kmer lengths directly:

```
for kmer_length in args.kmer_length:
    print("Counting kmers of length " + str(kmer_length))
    ...
```

As expected, the usage message changes to show that the -k flag can take multiple values separated by spaces:

```
usage: find_kmers_multiple.py [-h] [-k [KMER_LENGTH [KMER_LENGTH ...]]] [-t THRESHOLD] [-p] input_filename
```

This is how we run the program:

```
$ python find_kmers_multiple.py -k 2 3 6 -p dna.txt
Counting kmers of length 2
...
Counting kmers of length 3
...
Counting kmers of length 6
...
```

but note that we run into a problem if we swap the order of the arguments and put the kmer lengths immediately before the input file name:

```
$ python find_kmers_multiple.py -p -k 2 3 4 dna.txt
...
test.py: error: argument -k/--kmer_length: invalid check_kmer_length value: 'dna.txt'
```

Chapter 6:Building user interfaces

Our argument parser has assumed that the last part of the command line (dna.txt) was part of the list of kmer lengths. To get round this, we could make the input file name a flag argument as well (note that we should also make it a required argument, since the program can't run without it):

```
parser.add_argument(
    "-i",
    "--input_filename",
    help="the name of your DNA sequence file",
    required=True
    )
```

This removes any ambiguity because the command line now becomes:

```
$ python example.py -p -k 2 3 4 -i dna.txt
```

Multiple choice options

Let's add a couple more output options to our program. Imagine we want the user to be able to ask for the kmer frequencies to be displayed as raw counts, proportions (i.e. between 0 and 1) or percentages (i.e. between 0 and 100). We could quite easily do this with the tools we've seen so far: just add a new command line argument:

```
parser.add_argument(
    "-o",
    "--output_type",
    default = 'proportion'
    )
```

and then use the value of that option to decide what to do when printing a kmer whose count is above the threshold:

```
...
for kmer, count in kmer_counts.items():
        fraction = count / total_count
        if fraction > args.threshold:
            if args.output_type == 'proportion':
                print(kmer, count / total_count)
            elif args.output_type == 'percentage':
                print(kmer, (count / total_count) * 100)
            elif args.output_type == 'count':
                print(kmer, count)
```

This approach works fine, as long as we supply a value for -o that's one of the three valid options – here's what happens when we run our program with the same input file and parameters but different output types:

```
$ python example.py -p -k 4 -i dna.txt -o proportion
...
('AAAT', 0.017728834018816763)
...

$ python example.py -p -k 4 -i dna.txt -o percentage
...
('AAAT', 1.7728834018816764)
...

$ python example.py -p -k 4 -i dna.txt -o count
...
('AAAT', 271034)
...
```

However, problems arise when we ask for an invalid output type:

```
$ python example.py -k 4 -i dna.txt -o fraction
Counting kmers of length 4
```

Rather than getting an error message, the program runs but doesn't produce any output, because none of the three conditions in the code above is true. This is dangerous, as a user could interpret the output as meaning that there aren't any frequently occuring kmers in the input sequence.

Chapter 6:Building user interfaces

Unfortunately, the usage and help messages don't give us any hint of what output types are available:

```
$ python example.py -h
usage: example.py [-h] -i INPUT_FILENAME [-k [KMER_LENGTH
[KMER_LENGTH ...]]] [-t THRESHOLD] [-p] [-o OUTPUT_TYPE]
```

Rather than adding extra text and a custom validation function to deal with this problem, we can instead take advantage of `argparse`'s support for choices. We simply add a `choices` keyword argument to the `add_argument()` method, listing the allowed values for the `output_type` argument:

```
parser.add_argument(
    "-o",
    "--output_type",
    choices=['count', 'proportion', 'percentage'],
    default = 'proportion'
)
```

find_kmers_choices.py

This causes `argparse` to take care of adding the allowable options to the usage and help messages:

```
usage: find_kmers_choices.py ... [-o {count,proportion,percentage}]
```

as well as reminding the user of the options if they supply a value that isn't one of the choices:

```
$ python find_kmers_choices.py -k 4 -i dna.txt -o fraction
error: argument -o/--output_type: invalid choice: 'fraction' (choose from
'count', 'proportion', 'percentage')
```

Mutually exclusive options

Now that we have the ability to display the kmer frequencies as either counts, proportions or percentages, perhaps we should allow the user to specify the threshold in the same three ways. We can use three different command line arguments to do this:

```
parser.add_argument(
    "--proportion_threshold",
    help="minimum proportion of a kmer to be printed (between 0 and 1)",
    type=float
    )

parser.add_argument(
    "--percentage_threshold",
    help="minimum percentage of a kmer to be printed (between 0 and 100)",
    type=float
    )

parser.add_argument(
    "--count_threshold",
    help="minimum count of a kmer to be printed (positive integer)",
    type=int
    )
```

For clarity, we're just using long form arguments in the above code, and not doing any clever validation. Using these arguments in the code is a little bit more complicated than our previous examples: we have to convert the threshold supplied by the user into a minimum count:

```
# figure out the count threshold
if args.count_threshold is not None:
    print("Using count threshold " + str(args.count_threshold))
    count_threshold = args.count_threshold

elif args.proportion_threshold is not None:
    print("Using proportion threshold " + str(args.proportion_threshold))
    count_threshold = total_count * args.proportion_threshold

elif args.percentage_threshold is not None:
    print("Using percentage threshold " + str(args.percentage_threshold))
    count_threshold = total_count * (args.percentage_threshold / 100)
```

and then use that minimum count to decide which kmers to print:

Chapter 6:Building user interfaces

```
for kmer, count in kmer_counts.items():
    if count > count_threshold:
        ...
```

This works fine; we can now express the threshold for printing kmers in various different ways:

```
$ python example.py --proportion_threshold 0.01 dna.txt
Counting kmers of length 4
Using proportion threshold 0.01
('AAAT', 0.017728834018816763)
...

$ python example.py --percentage_threshold 2 dna.txt
Counting kmers of length 4
Using percentage threshold 2.0
('AAAA', 0.029265913606259023)
...

$ python example.py --count_threshold 300000 dna.txt
Counting kmers of length 4
Using count threshold 300000
('AAAA', 0.029265913606259023)
...
```

Notice that in the examples above, although we're specifying the threshold in different ways, we're using the default value for the `ouput_type` argument, so the kmer frequencies are always being displayed as proportions.

The problem with this approach is that it's now possible for the user to give conflicting instructions to the program. What should we do if there are two incompatible thresholds given?

```
$ python example.py  --count_threshold 300000 --proportion_threshold 0.05 dna.txt
```

Currently, our program will simply ignore the second threshold argument. What we need is some way of telling `argparse` that the three threshold arguments are mutually exclusive – the user isn't allowed to use more than

Chapter 6: Building user interfaces

one. Doing this is very straightforward: we create a mutually exclusive group object and add the arguments to the group rather than to the parser object:

```
threshold_group = parser.add_mutually_exclusive_group()

threshold_group.add_argument(
    "--proportion_threshold",
    help="minimum proportion of a kmer to be printed (between 0 and 1)",
    type=float
)

threshold_group.add_argument(
    "--percentage_threshold",
    help="minimum percentage of a kmer to be printed (between 0 and 100)",
    type=float
)

threshold_group.add_argument(
    "--count_threshold",
    help="minimum count of a kmer to be printed (positive integer)",
    type=int
)
```
find_kmers_thresholds.py

Now supplying more than one threshold argument results in a helpful error message:

```
$ python find_kmers_thresholds.py  --count_threshold 300000
    --proportion_threshold 0.05 dna.txt
error: argument --proportion_threshold: not allowed
    with argument --count_threshold
```

and we don't have to make any changes to the rest of the code.

Given that it doesn't make any sense for the program to run without a threshold, we should finish this modification by either adding a default value to one of the threshold options:

Chapter 6:Building user interfaces

```
threshold_group.add_argument(
    "--proportion_threshold",
    help="minimum proportion of a kmer to be printed (between 0 and 1)",
    type=float,
    default = 0.01
    )
```

or making the threshold group required:

```
threshold_group = parser.add_mutually_exclusive_group(required=True)
```

which will cause a helpful error message to be printed if the user doesn't give a threshold:

```
$ python find_kmers_thresholds.py dna.txt
error: one of the arguments --proportion_threshold
    --percentage_threshold --count_threshold is required
```

For details of many more things we can do with the `argparse` module, take a look at the documentation[1] and tutorial[2].

Alternatives to argparse

When building user interfaces, it's logical that the Python standard library (and hence `argparse`) will be our first stop. After all, the goal of a user interface is to make our program easier to use, so requiring the user to go through the extra step of installing another command line parsing library seems counterproductive.

However, for more complicated programs, the extra step might be justified if it allows you – the programmer – to manage the user interface better. We should at least consider other modules.

---

1   https://docs.python.org/2.7/library/argparse.html
2   https://docs.python.org/2/howto/argparse.html

click

The `click` module[1] is a mature project which offers very concise ways to build command line interfaces through decorators. As well as implementing all the types of command line argument parsing logic we have discussed above, it also has a bunch of useful features for more advanced command line interfaces. For example, it can mix command line and interactive prompts, hide passwords while the user is typing them, and produce output in multiple colours.

The documentation for `click` is excellent, so if you want to do something that `argparse` doesn't easily allow, I strongly recommend you check it out. In particular, if you want to write a command line interface that allows *commands* (i.e. instructions that make the program carry out different jobs) as well as just *options*, it's a great solution.

docopt

Another module worthy of note is `docopt`, which takes an unusual approach to designing command line interfaces[2]. Most tools – including `argparse` and `click` – allow you to specify options and then take care of generating a help message based on the options you described. With `docopt` it works the other way around: you write the help message (following certain conventions) and from that, `docopt` works out what the allowable options are. This may be a good choice if you're already very familiar with command line help conventions.

---

1 http://click.pocoo.org/5/
2 https://github.com/docopt/docopt

curses

Sometimes we need a command line interface that behaves a bit more graphically. In other words, one that allows us to draw windows in different parts of the terminal, to implement menus, and to update different parts of the screen while the program is running. This is very tricky to do with just the `print()` function – if you've ever tried to, for example, display a nicely formatted table with `print()` you'll know that it involves quite a bit of logic.

For these kinds of "graphical command line interfaces", the best place to start is with the `curses`[1] module. It's part of the Python standard library, and contains many useful functions for drawing windows, getting input and formatting output.

Configuration files

So far in this chapter we've been discussing user interfaces, in general terms, as ways to get information from the user. Another way of getting information from the user is to store it in a configuration file.

Configuration files have several advantages over an interactive or command line interface. The user can decide on their options once rather than having to enter them each time they run a program, and for large projects it's convenient to have all the options stored in one place.

The disadvantage, of course, is that changing an option is a more involved process; the user will have to locate the configuration file on disk, open it, and edit the bit of information they want to change. In this respect, having the user give options in a configuration file is a bit like having them edit the code – although obviously configuration files are much easier to navigate.

---

[1]   https://docs.python.org/2/library/curses.html

Writing configuration files in Python

Because Python's syntax is so simple, we can implement a configuration file simply by making a Python module that stores the required variables. Let's go back to the simplest version of our kmer counting program from the start of the chapter:

```python
input_filename = "dna.txt"
kmer_length = 4
threshold = 0.01

dna = open(input_filename).read().rstrip("\n")
all_kmers = []
for start in range(len(dna) - kmer_length + 1):
    kmer = dna[start:start+kmer_length]
    all_kmers.append(kmer)

kmer_counts = collections.Counter(all_kmers)
total_count = len(all_kmers)

for kmer, count in kmer_counts.items():
    fraction = count / total_count
    if fraction > threshold:
        print(kmer, count, fraction)
```

find_kmers.py

and create a configuration file for it. We'll create a new file called *kmer_config.py* and save it in the same folder. Inside the new file we'll put the first three lines from our original code:

```python
input_filename = "dna.txt"
kmer_length = 4
threshold = 0.01
```

kmer_config.py

and we'll delete these lines from the original code and import the newly created file:

Chapter 6:Building user interfaces

```
import kmer_config

dna = open(kmer_config.input_filename).read().rstrip("\n")
all_kmers = []
for start in range(len(dna) - kmer_config.kmer_length + 1):
    kmer = dna[start:start+kmer_config.kmer_length]
    all_kmers.append(kmer)

kmer_counts = collections.Counter(all_kmers)
total_count = len(all_kmers)

for kmer, count in kmer_counts.items():
    fraction = count / total_count
    if fraction > kmer_config.threshold:
        print(kmer, count, fraction)
```

`find_kmers_config_file.py`

Notice how we have to prefix all references to variables from the configuration file with the module name (i.e. `kmer_length` becomes `kmer_config.kmer_length`).

We now have a nice separation between code and options. If the user wants to change the input file name, kmer length or threshold they can edit the *kmer_config.py* file – the meaning of the different options are fairly obvious from the variable names, and the user doesn't even need to know that what they're editing is actually Python code.

When we use a configuration file in this way it's usual to add some documentation to the file for the user to read while they are editing it, which we can easily do with comments:

Chapter 6: Building user interfaces

```
# path to the input file name, which must contain a DNA sequence
input_filename = "dna.txt"

# length of kmers to analyse - must be a positive integer
kmer_length = 4

# minimum proportion of the sequence that a kmer must represent
# must be a floating point number between 0 and 1
threshold = 0.01
```

Because the configuration file is just Python code, we can add list and boolean options quite easily:

```
# path to the input file name, which must contain a DNA sequence
input_filename = "dna.txt"

# a list of kmer lengths to analyse, separated with commas
# each number must be a positive integer
# don't remove the square brackets!
kmer_lengths = [4,5,8]

# minimum proportion of the sequence that a kmer must represent
# must be a floating point number between 0 and 1
threshold = 0.01

# change this to False if you don't want to see the progress bar
show_progressbar = True
```

kmer_config_advanced.py

and simply refer to the variables inside the code. To avoid having to type `kmer_config_advanced` all the time, we'll use a short alias❶ :

Chapter 6:Building user interfaces

```
import kmer_config_advanced as cfg  ❶

dna = open(cfg.input_filename).read().rstrip("\n")

for kmer_length in cfg.kmer_lengths:
    print("Counting kmers of length " + str(kmer_length))
    all_kmers = []

    if cfg.show_progressbar:
        iterable = tqdm(range(len(dna) - kmer_length + 1))
    else:
        iterable = range(len(dna) - kmer_length + 1)

    for start in iterable:
        kmer = dna[start:start+kmer_length]
        all_kmers.append(kmer)

    kmer_counts = collections.Counter(all_kmers)
    total_count = len(all_kmers)

    for kmer, count in kmer_counts.items():
        fraction = count / total_count
        if fraction > cfg.threshold:
            print(kmer, count, fraction)
```

find_kmers_advanced_config_file.py

A nice aspect of the configuration file approach is that it gives us a very natural way to implement default values: if we write and distribute a sample configuration file along with our program, then we can populate it with default values which users can then change if they wish.

ConfigParser

The `ConfigParser`[1] (changed to `configparser` in Python 3 – note the different capitalization) module handles configuration files with a slightly more complicated structure. Here's what our configuration file would look like in this structure:

---

1 https://docs.python.org/2/library/configparser.html

```
[input]
# path to the input file name, which must contain a DNA sequence
input_filename:dna.txt

[analysis]
# a list of kmer lengths to analyse, separated with commas
# each number must be a positive integer
kmer_lengths:4,5,8

# minimum proportion of the sequence that a kmer must represent
# must be a floating point number between 0 and 1
threshold:0.01

[output]
# change this to False if you don't want to see the progress bar
show_progressbar:True
```

There are quite a few changes relative to our simple Python configuration file:

- Options are now grouped into sections, each of which starts with the option name in square brackets (`[input]`, `[analysis]`, etc.). This means that we can have multiple options with the same name, as long as they are in different sections.

- Option names and their values are separated by colons rather than equals signs

- Because this is now a plain text file rather than Python code, we don't need quotation marks around strings like the input file name

- The `kmer_lengths` option is no longer a list, but a simple string with numbers separated by commas.

To use this configuration file in our code, we create a `ConfigParser` object and ask it to read the configuration file:

Chapter 6:Building user interfaces

```
import ConfigParser

config = ConfigParser.RawConfigParser()
config.read("kmers.config")
```

To get a value from the file, we use the `get()` method on our `ConfigParser` object and give it the section and option we're looking for:

```
input_filename = config.get("input", "input_filename")
```

The value that `get()` returns is always a string. If we want to retrieve a floating point number – for instance, the threshold – we have to use `getfloat()` instead:

```
threshold = config.getfloat("analysis", "threshold")
```

There's also a `getboolean()` which will help us determine whether or not to display the progress bar:

```
show_progressbar = config.getboolean("output", "show_progressbar")
```

For the list of kmer lengths it's a bit more complicated: we can't just use the `getint()` method because we want a list of integers rather than a single integer. Instead we have to get the value as a string, split it into a list of strings, then convert each string to an integer before using it:

```
kmer_lengths = config.get("analysis", "kmer_lengths").split(",")

for kmer_length in kmer_lengths:
    kmer_length = int(kmer_length)
    ...
```

Configuration files written in this way, rather than as simple Python modules, are easier for the user to edit but require more work for the programmer. The `ConfigParser` module also allows programs to write configuration data to a file – see the documentation for an example[1] – which isn't easy with the pure Python approach.

In some situations it might make sense to store configuration data in another format. If the configuration data is very hierarchical, you might consider using JSON[2] format, which can be created and parsed with the `json` module[3] from the standard library. This approach might also be useful if your configuration options need to be parsed or written by other programs.

Of course, there's nothing to stop you inventing your own configuration file format and writing custom code to parse it, but this is likely to be far more time consuming than using one of the standard options!

Web interfaces

If you've done any bioinformatics work in the past then you've probably used analysis tools via a web interface. Online versions of tools are common, from complex algorithms like like BLAST for sequence similarity search[4] and Clustal for multiple sequence alignment[5], to simple tools for calculating codon usage[6] and plotting amino acid residue frequency[7].

The reasoning behind building online interfaces to tools can differ from case to case. Sometimes it's simply to allow users to make use of a tool without having to install it (this is especially true for tools that have a lot of tricky dependencies). Sometimes it's to allow users to make use of powerful servers to run jobs that would take a long time on desktop

---

1   https://docs.python.org/2/library/configparser.html#examples
2   http://json.org/
3   https://docs.python.org/2/library/json.html
4   http://blast.ncbi.nlm.nih.gov/Blast.cgi
5   http://www.ebi.ac.uk/Tools/msa/clustalo/
6   http://www.bioinformatics.nl/cgi-bin/emboss/cusp
7   http://www.bioinformatics.nl/cgi-bin/emboss/freak

machines (Clustal might fall into this category) or to avoid users having to download large datasets (as is the case for BLAST).

Any or all of these factors might be relevant to your programs. Alternatively, you might choose to write a web interface to take advantage of the many excellent libraries for visualization that run in the browser. Surprisingly, the explosion of interest in web development means that, in many cases, the quickest way to build an easy-to-use graphical interface is by building a web interface. The fact that such an interface makes your program usable from around the world becomes a bonus.

Developing web applications is a massive topic, and any in depth discussion of it requires detailed descriptions of how web technologies work, which is well beyond the scope of this book, so we'll just take a quick look at a very simple example.

A simple web interface using bottle

It is possible to build a web interface for your program using just the Python standard library – the place to start looking would be the `cgi` module[1]. However, doing so is extremely painful: there's a lot of tedious housekeeping involved in running web servers, capturing data from forms, etc. Instead, we're going to use a *web framework*.

A web framework is simply a module that makes it easier for us to build a web interface by handling many of the details. This lets us get up and running much quicker, and allows us to concentrate on the details of our program rather than the generalities of web programming.

For this example, we'll use `bottle`[2], a lightweight web framework that will take care of serving our web pages, getting input from the user, and

---

1   https://docs.python.org/2/library/cgi.html
2   http://bottlepy.org/docs/dev/index.html

displaying the output. If you want to try running the examples you'll have to install it by running

```
$ pip install bottle
```

Our web interface will have two pages: one for collecting the input and one for presenting the output. We'll start by figuring out what the input page should look like. We want to make a form with three fields: the DNA sequence[1], the kmer length and the threshold. The HTML for our form looks like this:

```
<form action="/output" method="post">
 DNA: <input name="dna" type="text" /><br/>
 kmer length: <input name="kmer_length" type="text" /><br/>
 threshold: <input name="threshold" type="text" /><br/>
 <input value="Analyse" type="submit" />
</form>
```

If you're not familiar with HTML then don't worry about the details. We are just describing a form that has text fields called dna, kmer_length and threshold, and a button marked "Analyse". When the user fills in the form and presses the button, it will submit it to the URL /output. If we were to save this text in a file and open it in a web browser, this is what it would look like with the values filled in:

---

[1] For a real life web interface to our program we would rather get the user to upload a file containing the DNA sequence, but that would make our example too complicated.

Chapter 6:Building user interfaces

Having written our HTML, we can now write a function that returns it as a string:

```
def kmers_form():
    return '''
        <form action="/output" method="post">
            DNA: <input name="dna" type="text" /><br/>
            kmer length: <input name="kmer_length" type="text" /><br/>
            threshold: <input name="threshold" type="text" /><br/>
            <input value="Analyse" type="submit" />
        </form>
    '''
```

find_kmers_bottle.py

Surrounding the string with three quotation marks allows us to split it over multiple lines[1]. To get this function to run as part of our web interface, we add a `@route` decorator which gives the path where we want to display it – in this case, /input:

```
from bottle import route, run

@route('/input')
def kmers_form():
    return '''
        <form action="/output" method="post">
            DNA: <input name="dna" type="text" /><br/>
            kmer length: <input name="kmer_length" type="text" /><br/>
            threshold: <input name="threshold" type="text" /><br/>
            <input value="Analyse" type="submit" />
        </form>
    '''
```

find_kmers_bottle.py

Note that we had to import this `@route` decorator from the `bottle` module. To actually start the web application running, we use the `run()`

---

[1] If you know HTML, then you're probably aware that this `<form>` element is not, by itself, a valid web page. Let's not worry about that for now; our web browser will be able to fill in the missing bits.

function (which we also imported) and pass in the name of the server (in this case `localhost`, which just means the computer we're currently working on) and the port (the number that goes after the server name in the URL). We also pass in the `debug` argument so that we get helpful output:

```
run(host='localhost', port=8080, debug=True)
```

Running this program tells us what the address is:

```
Bottle v0.12.9 server starting up (using WSGIRefServer())...
Listening on http://localhost:8080/
```

and if we type the address `http://localhost:8080/input` in our web browser, we will indeed see our input form (try it!). Trying to submit the form, unsurprisingly, results in an error, because we haven't written the second part of our interface yet.

The second function will retrieve the information that the user entered in the form – it's effectively doing the same job as the command line parser or the configuration file parser from earlier in the chapter. Thanks to `bottle`, this is quite easy: we call `request.forms.get()` for each bit of information we need and pass in the name of the field from the form:

```
dna = request.forms.get('dna')
kmer_length = int(request.forms.get('kmer_length'))
threshold = float(request.forms.get('threshold'))
```

As we should be used to by now, the values are returned as strings, so we have to explicitly convert them to integers and floats. From here on, the code can proceed as normal, with one slight difference: rather than printing the output, we want to store it in a variable so we can return it. To do this we'll create an empty result string❶ and append a single line where we would normally print a line❷:

Chapter 6:Building user interfaces

```
def count_kmers():
    # get the form parameters
    dna = request.forms.get('dna')
    kmer_length = int(request.forms.get('kmer_length'))
    threshold = float(request.forms.get('threshold'))

    # construct the result
    result = "" ❶
    all_kmers = []

    for start in range(len(dna) - kmer_length + 1):
        kmer = dna[start:start+kmer_length]
        all_kmers.append(kmer)

    kmer_counts = collections.Counter(all_kmers)
    total_count = len(all_kmers)


    for kmer, count in kmer_counts.items():
        fraction = count / total_count
        if fraction > threshold:
            line = kmer + "," + str(count) + "," + str(fraction) + "<br/>"❷
            result = result + line
    return result
```

find_kmers_bottle.py

Notice that our output lines end with the string `"<br/>"` – this is the HTML equivalent of a new line. Finally, we need to hook this function up to the rest of the program by adding the `@post` decorator (we use `@post` rather than `@route` because we only want this function to run when the user has submitted a form):

```
@post('/output')
def count_kmers():
    ...
```

We can test our web interface by restarting the program, pointing our browser at `http://localhost:8080/input`, filling in the form and pressing the "Analyse" button. The output is displayed in the web browser:

Chapter 6:Building user interfaces

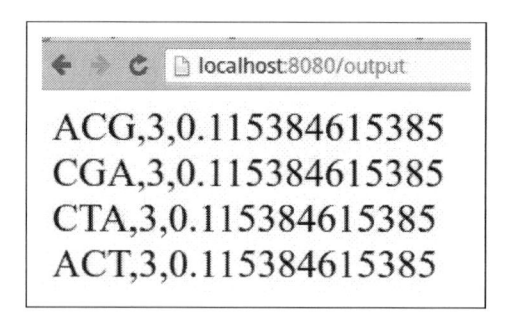

```
localhost:8080/output
ACG,3,0.115384615385
CGA,3,0.115384615385
CTA,3,0.115384615385
ACT,3,0.115384615385
```

There's obviously a lot missing from this minimal example. Before we put this tool on the web for our colleagues to use, we'd want to add input validation, make it look a bit better with some styling, perhaps format the output as a proper HTML table, and add the other output and input options that we had in the command line interface. The `bottle` documentation[1] is probably the best place to start reading if you think this type of thing might be useful.

There are a number of other Python web frameworks worth noting. The `flask` module[2] fills a similar role to `bottle` (hence the names). The `cherrypy` module[3] does the same thing but in a more object oriented way[4]. There are also more heavyweight solutions: web frameworks which handle things like interactions with databases, security and user accounts, and HTML templates. The most well known is probably Django[5]; also check out TurboGears[6].

---

1   http://bottlepy.org/docs/dev/index.html
2   http://flask.pocoo.org/
3   http://www.cherrypy.org/
4   The chapter on object-oriented programming in Advanced Python for Biologists may be helpful if you decide to try this one out.
5   https://www.djangoproject.com/
6   http://www.turbogears.org/

Chapter 6:Building user interfaces

If you've written a program that's useful specifically in a bioinformatics context, then another option is to consider integrating it into an existing web based platform. The most well known is currently the Galaxy[1] project, which is widely used and has a straightforward process for integrating new tools[2].

Graphical user interfaces

It's pretty rare that a graphical user interface is the best option in bioinformatics work. Graphical user interfaces have all of the drawbacks of interactive interfaces that we discussed before: they are hard to automate and their use can't easily be documented. In addition, graphical user interfaces are **very** time consuming to make. It takes a lot of time even to come up with a good design for a graphical interface, even before you factor in the time required to write the code.

If, however, you find yourself in the position of having to build a graphical user interface for a Python program, the choice of module is easy: `Tkinter` (renamed `tkinter` in Python 3) is part of the Python standard library and works without difficulty on most operating systems. Let's look at how to build a simple graphical interface for our kmer counting program using `Tkinter`.

Labels and fields

The design for our interface will be somewhat similar to the web interface: we need three text entry fields, each with a label telling the user what it is. We start by importing the `Tkinter` module, then calling the `Tk()` function to create an object that represents the window of our interface:

---

1   https://galaxyproject.org/
2   https://wiki.galaxyproject.org/Admin/Tools/AddToolTutorial

Chapter 6:Building user interfaces

```
import Tkinter
window = Tkinter.Tk()
```

We then call the `Label()` function to create a label object (passing in the window object as an argument along with the text that we want the label to display). To actually display the label, we call its `pack()` method, which causes `Tkinter` to add it to the window:

```
dna_label = Tkinter.Label(window, text="Enter DNA sequence:")
dna_label.pack()
```

We do the same with the `Entry()` function to create a text entry object:

```
dna_entry = Tkinter.Entry(window)
dna_entry.pack()
```

Finally, we call the `mainloop()` method on our window object which starts our application running:

```
window.mainloop()
```

Running this code gives us a very minimal interface: a window with a text label and a space to enter a DNA sequence:

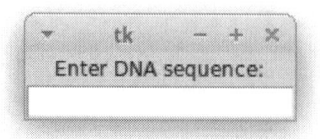

We can add similar labels and text entry spaces for the kmer length and threshold by repeating the `Label()` and `Entry()` functions:

Chapter 6:Building user interfaces

```
kmer_length_label = Tkinter.Label(window, text="Enter kmer length:")
kmer_length_label.pack()
kmer_length_entry = Tkinter.Entry(window)
kmer_length_entry.pack()

threshold_label = Tkinter.Label(window, text="Enter threshold:")
threshold_label.pack()
threshold_entry = Tkinter.Entry(window)
threshold_entry.pack()
```

find_kmers_tkinter_input.py

giving us an interface with three labels and three text fields:

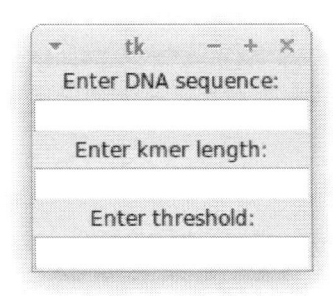

At this point we can fill in the text entry boxes, but not much else. To get the interface to actually do something, we need to add a button that can start our analysis running. First we have to write a function that will run when the button is pressed. For now, let's just print out the values of the three text entry boxes, which we can obtain using the `get()` method on the variables we created:

```
def analyse():
    print(dna_entry.get(), kmer_length_entry.get(), threshold_entry.get())
```

find_kmers_tkinter_button.py

To actually trigger this function, we'll create a button object using the `Button()` function. We have to pass several argument to the `Button()`

function: the name of the window variable, the text we want the button to display, the width, and the function that we want to run when the button is pressed (in our case, `analyse`):

```
analyse_button = Tkinter.Button(window,
                                text="Analyse",
                                width=10,
                                command=analyse)
analyse_button.pack()
```

find_kmers_tkinter_button.py

Just as with all the other elements of our interface, we must remember to call `pack()` to add the button to the window. The interface now looks like this:

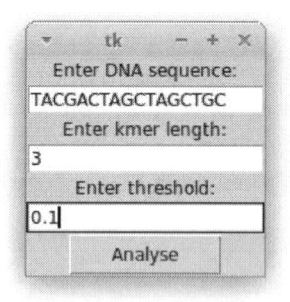

and if we fill in the values and press the "Analyse" button, we get the expected output:

```
('TACGACTAGCTAGCTGC', '3', '0.1')
```

At this point, we could add in the actual kmer counting code to our `analyse()` function and have it print the kmers to the command line, but

Chapter 6:Building user interfaces

we probably want the output to appear as part of the interface. To make space for the output, we'll need to create a text object by calling the `Text()` function. We supply a height and width argument to the `Text()` function to make sure that it's a sensible size:

```
output_text = Tkinter.Text(window, height=10, width=25)
output_text.pack()
```

find_kmers_tkinter_output.py

Let's test it by having our `analyse()` function display the three text values in the output area rather than the command line. We can add text to the output area by calling its `insert()` method:

```
def analyse():
    output_text.insert(Tkinter.END, dna_entry.get() + "\n")
    output_text.insert(Tkinter.END, kmer_length_entry.get() + "\n")
    output_text.insert(Tkinter.END, threshold_entry.get() + "\n")
```

In the above code, the first argument to `insert()` – `Tkinter.END` – is just a special value which instructs `Tkinter` to add the new text onto the end of the output. Initially the text output is empty:

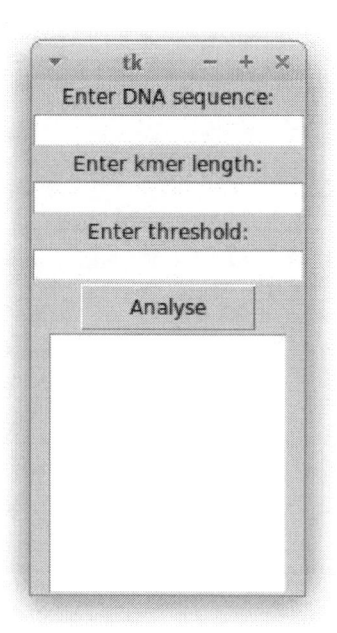

but once we fill in the text fields and press the "Analyse" button, the `analyse()` function runs and inserts the values in the boxes into the text output area:

Chapter 6:Building user interfaces

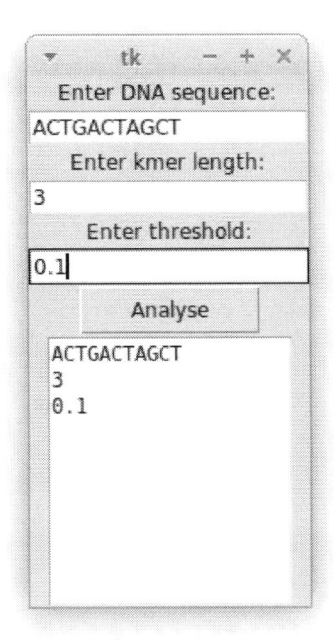

Now we can add in the kmer counting code to the `analyse()` function, being careful to first convert the kmer length and threshold values to the correct type:

Chapter 6:Building user interfaces

```
def analyse():
    # get the parameters ❶
    dna = dna_entry.get()
    kmer_length = int(kmer_length_entry.get())
    threshold = float(threshold_entry.get())

    all_kmers = []

    for start in range(len(dna) - kmer_length + 1):
        kmer = dna[start:start+kmer_length]
        all_kmers.append(kmer)

    kmer_counts = collections.Counter(all_kmers)
    total_count = len(all_kmers)

    for kmer, count in kmer_counts.items():
        proportion = count / total_count
        if proportion > threshold:
            line = kmer + "," + str(count) + "," + str(proportion) + "\n"
            output_text.insert(Tkinter.END, line) ❷
```

find_kmers_tkinter_final.py

The code that does the actual kmer counting is identical to the code at the start of the chapter. The only difference is in the first part of the function where we get the input variables❶, and in the output where we insert the kmers into the output text❷. Now when we fill in the values and press the "Analyse" button we get the usual kmer information in the output area:

Chapter 6:Building user interfaces

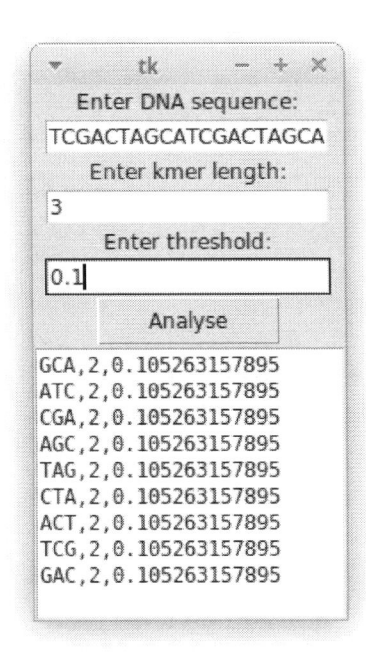

```
tk
Enter DNA sequence:
TCGACTAGCATCGACTAGCA
Enter kmer length:
3
Enter threshold:
0.1
        Analyse
GCA,2,0.105263157895
ATC,2,0.105263157895
CGA,2,0.105263157895
AGC,2,0.105263157895
TAG,2,0.105263157895
CTA,2,0.105263157895
ACT,2,0.105263157895
TCG,2,0.105263157895
GAC,2,0.105263157895
```

Let's finish by making a few small improvements. We would like the user to be able to run the program, then make some changes to the input text and rerun the analysis (e.g. by changing the kmer length). If we do this with our current code, the new output will just be added on to the end of the old output, so we won't be able to see it. To fix this we can delete any existing output text each time we run the `analyse()` function:

```
def analyse():
    output_text.delete("1.0", Tkinter.END)
    ...
```

find_kmers_tkinter_polished.py

The `delete()` method removes all the text from the position given by the first argument to the position given by the second argument. The reason for the strange looking start position `"1.0"` is that it's specifying a column

Chapter 6:Building user interfaces

and row – the zeroth column of the first row, which just means the very start of the text.

Next, let's try using a couple of different elements for inputting the different variables. For the threshold we can use a slider object, which we create by calling the `Scale()` function. We want our slider to go from 0 to 1 in steps of 0.01, and to be displayed horizontally (side to side) rather than vertically:

```
threshold_label = Tkinter.Label(window, text="Enter threshold:")
threshold_label.pack()

threshold_entry = Tkinter.Scale(
    window,
    from_=0,
    to=1,
    orient=Tkinter.HORIZONTAL,
    resolution=0.01)

threshold_entry.pack()
```

<code>find_kmers_tkinter_polished.py</code>

Notice how the keyword `from_` in the arguments to `Tkinter.Scale()` ends with an underscore – that's because the word `from` already has a special meaning in Python. This is what our interface looks like with the slider:

Chapter 6:Building user interfaces

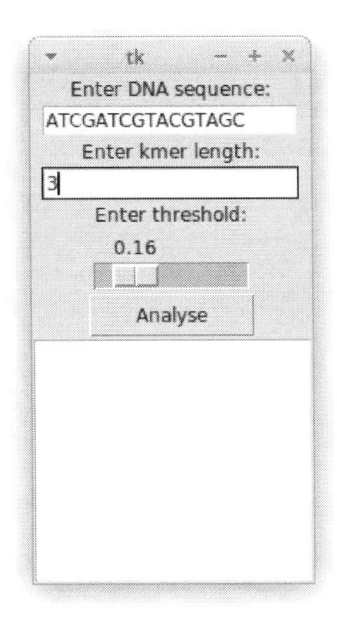

This is easier for the user than typing in a text box, but also makes life easier for the programmer. Because the `get()` method on a slider object returns a floating point number (unlike the `get()` method on a text box, which always returns a string) we don't have to explicitly convert it. It also makes input validation much easier[1], as it's now impossible for the user to enter something for the threshold that isn't a valid floating point number.

Can we do something similar with the kmer length? We could just use another slider, if we're prepared to manually pick a maximum kmer length:

---

1   For clarity, we've not been doing any input validation in this example, but we would in real life.

Chapter 6:Building user interfaces

```
kmer_length_entry = Tkinter.Scale(
    window,
    from_=1,
    to=20,
    orient=Tkinter.HORIZONTAL,
    resolution=1)

kmer_length_entry.pack()
```

remembering to change the resolution to one, since the kmer length needs to be an integer. Alternatively, since the kmer length values are discrete rather than continuous it might make more sense to use a spinbox:

```
kmer_length_entry = Tkinter.Spinbox(window, from_=1, to=20)
kmer_length_entry.pack()
```

find_kmers_tkinter_polished.py

which allows the user to either type a value, or increase or decrease it by clicking the arrows:

Chapter 6:Building user interfaces

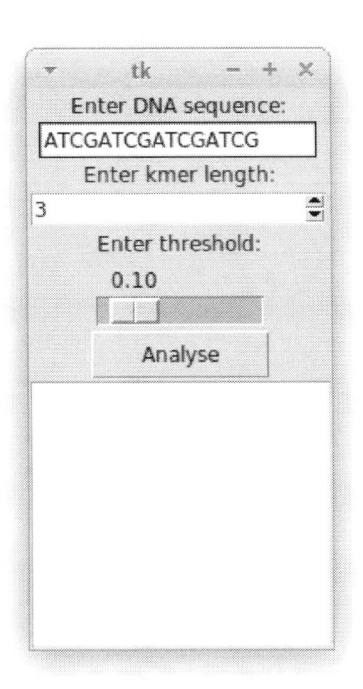

Hopefully this minimal example has illustrated the benefits and drawbacks of building graphical user interfaces. You can see just by looking at the example code how much effort we have to devote to describing and laying out the interface. However, the addition of sliders, output boxes etc. undeniably allow us to present a friendlier interface to the user.

Logging

Typically when we write a Python program for scientific work we are interested in producing some output data, which generally goes to a file. However, our programs often produce other types of output as well – messages about what the program is doing, warnings that something has gone wrong, information about the state of variables, and error messages.

Here's a version of our kmer finding code that writes the frequently occurring kmers to a file rather than to the terminal:

Chapter 6:Building user interfaces

```
from __future__ import division
import collections
import sys

input_filename = sys.argv[1]    ❶
kmer_length = int(sys.argv[2])
count_threshold = int(sys.argv[3])
output_filename = sys.argv[4]

dna = open(input_filename).read().replace("\n", "")

kmer_counts = collections.Counter()

for start in range(len(dna) - kmer_length + 1):
    kmer = dna[start:start+kmer_length]
    kmer_counts.update([kmer])

total_count = sum(kmer_counts.values())

with open(output_filename, "w") as output:
    for kmer, count in kmer_counts.items():
        if count > count_threshold:
            output.write(kmer + " " + str(count) + "\n")
```

find_kmers_file_output.py

For simplicity, we're working with `sys.argv` for command line arguments❶, and not doing any input validation. The program takes four command line arguments – the name of a file that contains the DNA sequence; the kmer length; the minimum number of times a kmer has to occur to appear in the output, and the name of the output file to create. In this version the threshold and output are both based simply on absolute kmer counts rather than fractions or percentages.

If you run the program above you'll notice that it doesn't produce any output on the command line. Let's look at a version that is a bit more informative:

Chapter 6:Building user interfaces

```
input_filename = sys.argv[1]
...

if kmer_length < 1:
    print("kmer length must be positive")  ❶
    sys.exit()

if count_threshold < 100:
    print("warning: a low threshold produces a lot of output")  ❷

dna = open(input_filename).read().replace("\n", "")

kmer_counts = collections.Counter()

print("counting kmers of length " + str(kmer_length))  ❸
for start in range(len(dna) - kmer_length + 1):
    kmer = dna[start:start+kmer_length]
    kmer_counts.update([kmer])

total_count = sum(kmer_counts.values())

with open(output_filename, "w") as output:
    for kmer, count in kmer_counts.items():
        print("count for " + kmer + " is " + str(count))  ❹
        if count > count_threshold:
            output.write(kmer + " " + str(count) + "\n")
```

find_kmers_file_info.py

This version – which is more typical of programs that we use in the real world – is exactly the same, but with a few `print()` statements added. The interesting thing is that all these `print()` statements do slightly different jobs.

If the kmer length is invalid, we have a statement that will report an error before the program exits❶. If the count threshold is very low, then we will get a warning message about the volume of output❷ – note that this is not an error, because it doesn't actually prevent the program from continuing. Next, we have a line that simply prints the kmer length❸. This is neither an error nor a warning, but just a message informing the user about what

Chapter 6:Building user interfaces

the program is doing. Finally, we have a line that prints the count for every single kmer❹.

The problem with all of these different messages is that we want to see different combinations of them under different circumstances. When are working on the program, or trying to track down a bug, we want to see all the output, including the count for every kmer. However, in normal use we will probably comment out the line:

```
print("count for " + kmer + " is " + str(count))
```

as it produces a lot of output.

Similarly, if we end up running our program as part of an automated pipeline, we might want to suppress the message about the kmer length and any warnings about the threshold, and only see output that informs us about errors.

Obviously having to edit the code each time we want to change the level of detail we see is tedious, so we might be tempted to start adding flags to our program:

```
show_all_counts = True

...

with open(output_filename, "w") as output:
    for kmer, count in kmer_counts.items():
        if show_all_counts:
            print("count for " + kmer + " is " + str(count))
        if count > count_threshold:
            output.write(kmer + " " + str(count) + "\n")
```

If we do this, however, we'll find that the logic quickly starts cluttering up the code. A better approach is to take advantage of Python's logging system.

Chapter 6:Building user interfaces

Logging messages

To start, we simply import the `logging` module then change our `print()` statements to use the built in logging functions. From the most detailed to the least detailed these are `logging.debug()`, `logging.info()`, `logging.warning()` and `logging.critical()`.[1] Here's what our program looks like with the appropriate function calls:

```
import logging

...

if kmer_length < 1:
    logging.critical("kmer length must be positive")
    sys.exit()

if count_threshold < 100:
    logging.warning("a low threshold produces a lot of output")

dna = open(input_filename).read().replace("\n", "")

kmer_counts = collections.Counter()

logging.info("counting kmers of length " + str(kmer_length))

...

with open(output_filename, "w") as output:
    for kmer, count in kmer_counts.items():
        logging.debug("count for " + kmer + " is " + str(count))
        if count > count_threshold:
            output.write(kmer + " " + str(count) + "\n")
```

find_kmers_log.py

The only bits of code we have changed are the `print()` statements, and we have used different functions depending on their meaning:

---

[1] There's also a `logging.error()` for problems which cause some, but not all, of the program to stop working, but our program is too simple to require it.

- the error message about an invalid kmer length has become `logging.critical()`
- the warning about low thresholds has become `logging.warning()`
- the message about the kmer length has become `logging.info()`
- the line which prints every kmer has become `logging.debug()`

How does this affect the output when we run the program? By default, logging is set up to only print messages of warning or critical. So if we run with an invalid kmer length we'll see the error message:

```
$ python find_kmers_log.py small.dna -2 5000 test.out
CRITICAL:root:kmer length must be positive
```

and if we run with a small threshold we'll see the warning, but no further information:

```
$ python find_kmers_log.py small.dna 3 50 test.out
WARNING:root:a low threshold produces a lot of output
```

Notice how each message generated by logging is prefixed with its level. These are always written in upper case, so from now on we'll talk about DEBUG, INFO, WARNING and CRITICAL when discussing log messages. Each message is also prefixed by the word `root`; that's because it's possible to have multiple logs, but we don't need to worry about that now and can safely ignore it.

Seeing more information

If we want to see messages at the INFO or DEBUG levels, we need to configure the logger. We do this by adding a call to the `logger.basicConfig()` function at the start of our program and passing in a `level` keyword argument:

Chapter 6:Building user interfaces

```
logging.basicConfig(level=logging.INFO)
```

The different levels are defined in the `logging` module and use the upper case names described above. We can pick from `logging.DEBUG`, `logging.INFO`, `logging.WARNING` and `logging.CRITICAL`.

With `logging.CRITICAL` we suppress all output apart from catastrophic errors, so even with a very small threshold we don't get the warning message:

```
$ python find_kmers_log.py small.dna 3 50 test.out
$
```

This option is likely to be useful when running our program as part of an automated pipeline, where there is no human in place to read the warning.

With `logging.WARNING` we get the same behaviour as the default: we see messages at the CRITICAL and WARNING level but nothing below that:

```
$ python find_kmers_log.py small.dna 3 50 test.out
WARNING:root:a low threshold produces a lot of output
```

With `logging.INFO` we add in the messages that just tell us what the program is doing:

```
$ python find_kmers_log.py small.dna 3 50 test.out
WARNING:root:a low threshold produces a lot of output
INFO:root:counting kmers of length 3
```

and with `logging.DEBUG` we get all levels of output:

```
$ python find_kmers_log.py small.dna 3 50 test.out
WARNING:root:a low threshold produces a lot of output
INFO:root:counting kmers of length 3
DEBUG:root:count for CTT is 10598
DEBUG:root:count for ATG is 9410
...
```

Notice that we have achieved this level of flexibility without having to add any logic to our code – simply by categorizing our messages into the different levels, we can control what we see.

Logging to a file

In normal software development, logging serves a very important function: by providing a record of what happened during the execution of a program, it makes it easier to track down bugs and performance issues. In scientific work the same is true, but there's an extra benefit to logging: recording the execution of a piece of analysis allows us to go back and check the provenance of a particular result or piece of data. This can be useful in a variety of situations: maybe you need to double check the details of a particular bit of analysis before you make it the centrepiece of your paper, or maybe you need to look up the parameters of a program in order to repeat it with a different dataset.

To switch our program to use file logging, we just add a `filename` keyword argument to the `basicConfig()` function call:

```
logging.basicConfig(filename="test.log", level=logging.DEBUG)
```

Now any logging messages will be written to *test.log*.

For a more complex program we might want to have some messages written to a file and some displayed as output, with separate levels for each. Here's how to do it:

```
logging.basicConfig(filename="test.log", level=logging.DEBUG)  ❶
console = logging.StreamHandler()  ❷
console.setLevel(logging.INFO)  ❸
logging.getLogger('').addHandler(console)  ❹
```

First we set up file logging as described above❶, then create a `StreamHandler` object❷ which will control the printing of messages to the console. We give the `StreamHandler` object its own level❸, which can be different from the file log level. Finally, we add the `StreamHandler` object to the list of logs❹.

In the above example, the *test.log* file will receive all messages, but only CRITICAL, ERROR, WARN and INFO messages will be printed (i.e. not DEBUG). Because we have two different logging levels, it might be convenient to break these out into dedicated variables:

```
file_logging_level = logging.DEBUG
print_logging_level = logging.INFO

logging.basicConfig(filename="test.log", level=file_logging_level)
console = logging.StreamHandler()
console.setLevel(print_logging_level)
logging.getLogger('').addHandler(console)
```

to make it easier to switch levels.

Standard output and standard error

When we run a program on the command line we actually get two types of output: standard output and standard error[1]. Most of the time this distinction doesn't matter, because both standard output and standard error get printed to the console. Sometimes, however, we wish to redirect output and only see errors, or vice versa.

By default, when we use the logging module our messages get written to standard error, which is normally the right thing to do. If we want to write our messages to standard output instead, we set the `stream` keyword argument in the `basicConfig()` function:

---

1   All command line programs behave this way, not just ones written in Python.

```
logging.basicConfig(stream=sys.stdout, level=logging.INFO)
```

We can also have separate levels for standard error and standard output using a similar pattern to the one we saw above:

```
stdout_logging_level = logging.WARN
stderr_logging_level = logging.DEBUG

logging.basicConfig(stream=sys.stderr, level=stderr_logging_level)
console = logging.StreamHandler(stream=sys.stdout)
console.setLevel(stdout_logging_level)
logging.getLogger('').addHandler(console)
```

In this example, all messages will be written to standard error, but only WARN, ERROR and CRITICAL messages will be written to standard output. When using this pattern we have to make sure that the root logger (i.e. the one that we set using `basicConfig()`) has the lower level (DEBUG rather than WARN). Also, be aware that with this example, some messages will appear twice on the console as they will be written to both standard error and standard output.

Controlling verbosity

For tools that are intended to be used by non-programmers, editing the code to change the logging level is obviously not a great solution. In such cases it makes sense to have the logging level as one of the command line arguments.

The best way to implement this depends on how we are currently getting command line arguments. For our example we have simply been reading values from the `sys.argv` list. In the simplest case, we might offer the user a choice between two logging levels: one in which all messages are printed (i.e. with the logging level set to DEBUG) and one in which DEBUG messages are omitted (i.e. with the logging level set to INFO).

Chapter 6:Building user interfaces

Here's one way to implement such a flag:

```
input_filename = sys.argv[1]
kmer_length = int(sys.argv[2])
count_threshold = int(sys.argv[3])
output_filename = sys.argv[4]

if len(sys.argv) == 6 and sys.argv[5] == 'debug':
    logging.basicConfig(level=logging.DEBUG)
else:
    logging.basicConfig(level=logging.INFO)
```

Note that there is no validation for any of the command line arguments in our example – real world code will be more complex. In the above example, running the program with only four command line arguments triggers the default behaviour, which is to hide messages at the DEBUG level:

```
$ python example.py dna.txt 3 50 test.out
WARNING:root:a low threshold produces a lot of output
INFO:root:counting kmers of length 3
```

and running it with the debug command line argument triggers debugging mode:

```
$ python example.py dna.txt 3 50 test.out debug
WARNING:root:a low threshold produces a lot of output
INFO:root:counting kmers of length 3
DEBUG:root:count for CTT is 10598
DEBUG:root:count for ATG is 9410
...
```

For more fine grained control we might allow the user to specify any logging level:

```
if len(sys.argv) == 6 and sys.argv[5] == 'debug':
    logging.basicConfig(level=logging.DEBUG)
elif len(sys.argv) == 6 and sys.argv[5] == 'info':
    logging.basicConfig(level=logging.INFO)
elif len(sys.argv) == 6 and sys.argv[5] == 'warning':
    logging.basicConfig(level=logging.WARNING)
elif len(sys.argv) == 6 and sys.argv[5] == 'error':
    logging.basicConfig(level=logging.ERROR)
elif len(sys.argv) == 6 and sys.argv[5] == 'critical':
    logging.basicConfig(level=logging.CRITICAL)
```

although this number of levels is unlikely to be necessary for the majority of programs that we write.

A useful pattern when using the `argparse` module is to allow the user to specify the logging level by passing a particular command line argument (by convention -v, short for "verbose") a number of times. Here's how we might implement this for our program (for this example the input and output file names, kmer length and threshold are hard coded for simplicity):

```
parser = argparse.ArgumentParser()

parser.add_argument("-v", "--verbosity", action="count",
                    help="increase output verbosity")

args = parser.parse_args()

if args.verbosity == None:
    logging.basicConfig(level=logging.ERROR)
elif args.verbosity == 1:
    logging.basicConfig(level=logging.WARN)
elif args.verbosity == 2:
    logging.basicConfig(level=logging.INFO)
elif args.verbosity == 3:
    logging.basicConfig(level=logging.DEBUG)

input_filename = "dna.txt"
kmer_length = 3
count_threshold = 50
output_filename = "test.out"
```

Chapter 6:Building user interfaces

`find_kmers_log_options.py`

We add the argument to the parser with the `action` keyword set to `count`, then set the logging level depending on the number of times the `-v` argument was passed on the command line. Note that if there was no `-v` argument passed, the value of `args.verbosity` will be `None` rather than zero.

Let's take a look at how this works. With no `-v` argument we get only errors printed i.e. nothing is printed if the program runs successfully:

```
$ python find_kmers_log_options.py
$
```

With a single `-v` we add warnings:

```
$ python find_kmers_log_options.py -v
WARNING:root:a low threshold produces a lot of output
```

with two we add information messages:

```
$ python find_kmers_log_options.py -vv
WARNING:root:a low threshold produces a lot of output
INFO:root:counting kmers of length 3
```

and with three we add debugging information:

```
$ python find_kmers_log_options.py -vvv
WARNING:root:a low threshold produces a lot of output
INFO:root:counting kmers of length 3
DEBUG:root:count for CTT is 10598
DEBUG:root:count for ATG is 9410
DEBUG:root:count for AAG is 10148
...
```

We can also supply multiple separate `-v` arguments:

```
$ python find_kmers_log_options.py -v -v -v
WARNING:root:a low threshold produces a lot of output
INFO:root:counting kmers of length 3
DEBUG:root:count for CTT is 10598
DEBUG:root:count for ATG is 9410
DEBUG:root:count for AAG is 10148
...
```

and `argparse` will treat them just the same.

Adding time to our log messages

Often in bioinformatics work we end up writing programs that take a long time to run. For such programs it might be useful to have time stamp data in our log files – for example, we might want to look at the output of a long running program and see how long each step took. Doing this is relatively easy with the `logging` module, because we can supply a `format` string to the `basicConfig()` function specifying how we want our log messages to look. Within the format string we use the place holder `%(message)s` to refer to the actual message.

We can use this to add extra text to our log messages: a format string that looks like this:

```
logging.basicConfig(format="My program says: %(message)s")
```

will result in log messages that look like this:

```
My program says: a low threshold produces a lot of output
```

We can also use other place holders. The place holder `%(asctime)s` will insert the current date and time, so a format string like this:

```
logging.basicConfig(format="My program says: %(message)s at %(asctime)s")
```

will give us log messages that look like this:

Chapter 6:Building user interfaces

```
My program says: a low threshold produces a lot of output at 2016-05-13
10:20:45,653
```

These place holders are extremely powerful and allow us to insert all kinds of information into logging messages – everything from the function in which the message was created to the name of the Python file that is running. See the documentation[1] for a full list.

Recap

In this chapter we've looked at a number of different user interfaces to the same simple program. We've built a simple interactive interface; a simple and then more complex command line interfaces, a web interface and a graphical user interface.

Hopefully, looking at multiple interfaces to the same basic program has given you a feeling for the strengths and weaknesses of each approach. For most bioinformatics work, a command line interface is the best choice: it's most likely to fit in with other tools, it's amenable to automation, and you can document all the arguments used to run a program by simply copying and pasting the command line into a text file or an email.

Web and graphical user interfaces have their own specialized uses. If your program relies on huge datasets, building a web interface is pretty much the only way to avoid making users download them. A web interface can also be a good option for programs that have a lot of complicated dependencies[2]. If your program is intended to be used only by non-technical researchers who are unlikely to use the command line, then a

---

1   https://docs.python.org/2/library/logging.html#logrecord-attributes
2   But see also the section on containers and virtual machines in the chapter on programming environments for another solution to this problem.

graphical user interface is probably the most user friendly option – but be wary of the amount of time it can take to design, build and test it.

One final note: there's nothing to stop you doing exactly what we've done in this chapter and building multiple different user interfaces for a single tool. If you package your analysis code into a module[1] then it's quite straightforward to write multiple different user interfaces, each of which calls the same analysis code. This is a very common approach in bioinformatics; in fact, that's how all three of the tools mentioned at the start of the web interface section work – BLAST, Clustal and EMBOSS are all available both as web interfaces and as command line tools.

Printing information about the what's happening in a program is something that we do all the time when writing code. When our programs grow to a certain size and complexity, it makes sense to switch from simple `print()` statements to a more structured logging framework and, unsurprisingly, Python provides an excellent one as part of its standard library.

In this section we have touched on the basics of logging – including a couple of points specifically useful for bioinformatics – which will cover the majority of your logging needs for day to day scientific programming. Of course, there's far more that we can do with the logging framework. If you find yourself needing to do advanced tricks like sending logging messages across a network, keeping a rotating list of log files, or even having your computer dictate messages to you using text-to-speech, check out the logging module documentation[2] and cookbook[3].

---

1 See the chapter on packaging and sharing code.
2 https://docs.python.org/2/library/logging.html
3 https://docs.python.org/2/howto/logging-cookbook.html

Afterword

This is the end of *Effective Python development for biologists*; I hope you have enjoyed the book, and found it useful. Remember that if you have any comments on the book – good or bad – I'd love to hear them; drop me an email at

`martin@pythonforbiologists.com`

If you've found the book useful, please also consider leaving a Amazon **review**. Reviews will help other people to find the book, and hopefully make learning Python a bit easier for everyone.

Index

A
aliases 73
argparse 216
ArgumentTypeError 222
assert 88
assert_almost_equals() 124
assert_equal 108
assert_raises() 126
assertion 91
Atom 14

B
Benchmarking 140
biclustering 184
big O notation 157
BioPython 63
Boolean argument 229
bottle 251
breakpoint 46
bugjar 58
bugs 94

C
cffi 195
cgi 251
cherrypy 256
click 242
collections 65
collections.Counter 200
ConfigParser 247
Configuration files 243

Containers	23
continuous integration	136
cProfile	163
Creating a module	70
curses	243
Custom validation	222

D

dateutil	67
debuggers	25
Debugging exceptions	48
Default argument values	228
Docker	23
docopt	242
docstring	73

E

Emacs	14
epoch	141

F

fields	257
fixture	105
flask	256
floating point numbers	122
footnotes	6
formatting	5
functional tests	134

G

Galaxy	257
Gedit	13
graph-tool	185
graphical user interface	257
gzip	183

H
help message 220
helper function 130
HTML 253

I
IDE 14
IDLE 16
import 64
IndentationError 12
Input validation 210
input/output 181
integration tests 134
Ipdb 58
iPython 18

J
json 183, 250
Jupyter 18

K
kernprof 170

L
Labels 257
lambda expression 190
libraries 63
line_profiler 169
list comprehension 189
Logging 269
Logging to a file 276
long argument 225

M
map 189

matplotlib 18
memory usage 147
mock 134
mocking 134
module 62
Multiple choice options 235
multiprocessing 194
Mutually exclusive options 237

N

namespaces 71
nano 13
nose 105
nosetests 107
Notepad++ 13
Numba 196
NumPy 196

O

optional arguments 226
os module 149

P

package 62
Packages 79
pandas 18
parallelization 194
pdb 30
Pdb++ 58
pickle 183
pip 19
positional arguments 226
post_mortem 50
process id 149

Profiling.. 160
progress bar.. 205
psutil.. 149
Pudb.. 58
PyCharm... 17
PyPI... 81
PyPy.. 196
Python standard library.. 63

R
random.. 64
raw_input().. 203
readlines().. 182
Real time.. 141
realistic data.. 175
refactor... 15
refactoring... 97
regression.. 100
Relational Database Management Systems.......................... 195
resource module.. 147

S
Set up... 101
setup.py... 82
setuptools.. 83
short-circuiting.. 191
slider.. 266
spinbox.. 268
Spyder.. 17
sqlite3.. 196
standard error... 277
Standard output.. 277
step into... 55
Sublime Text.. 14

Syntax highlighting.. *12*
Sys time... *141*
sys.argv... *208*
sys.path... *65*

T
Tab emulation... *12*
tear down.. *101*
test suite.. *96*
test-driven development.. *136*
Testing exceptions.. *125*
testing object oriented code.. *131*
text editors.. *10*
TextWrangler.. *13*
time module... *142*
time stamp.. *282*
timeit... *142*
Tkinter... *257*
tqdm.. *205*
tuple... *190*
typography.. *5*

U
Unix time... *140*
upload.. *85*
usage.. *218*
user interface... *199*
user time... *141*

V
verbosity.. *278*
Vim... *14*
virtual appliance.. *25*
virtual environments... *19*

Virtual machines *24*
VirtualBox *25*
virtualenv *19*
virtualenvwrapper *21*

W
web framework *251*
web interface *251*
winpdb *58*
with_setup *115*

__init__.py *80*

_
__file__ *64*
__name__ *75*

Made in the USA
Charleston, SC
20 October 2016